JUSTICE CAN'T BE SERVED WHEN WE'VE GOT VENGEANCE ON OUR MIND

{SENTENCED FOR LIFE}

BY

Robert Davis

Unless otherwise noted, all scripture quotations are taken from the *King James Version* of the Bible.

Justice Can't Be Served When We've Got Vengeance On Our Mind.

ISBN-13: 978-1493699292 (CreateSpace-Assigned)
ISBN-10: 1493699296

First printing, December 2013

© 2010 Robert Davis

**Published by Joint Heirs to the Kingdom Publishing
2124 Ragan Woods Dr.
Toledo, Oh. 43614**

Printed in the United States of America. All rights reserved under International Copyright Law. Contents and/or cover may not be reproduced in whole or in part in any form without express written consent.

TABLE OF CONTENTS

Introduction

Chapter

1. Vengeance
2. Consequences
3. Disenfranchisement and Collateral Consequences
4. Marked
5. Vengeance the great Emasculator
6. Vengeance and the Media
7. Mental beat down
8. The abduction of Lady Justice
9. The Body of Justice
10. Laws for just us
11. Justice wins the peace
12. Justice Supreme

Conclusion

INTRODUCTION

"DON'T DO THE CRIME, IF YOU CAN'T DO THE TIME"! Sammy Davis Jr. immortalized the wisdom of these words in the theme song from the 70's hit television series Beretta. In other words; think before you act because there are consequences! The ultimate conformation of this truth is the lifelong effect that the criminal justice system has on people who have been convicted of a felony. From the time of your conviction, to the day that you take your last breath, in most cases the effect results in a life of mediocrity!

Regardless of the amount of potential that you possess or the seed of greatness that lies deep within; if you ever get or have ever been convicted of a felony in this country by default the criminal justice system will step into your life to stop the growth of that seed and hinder the development of that potential. This will make opportunities for advancement more difficult to attain because the system will use your past against you to try to stop you before you ever get started!

Those who did not take heed to the wisdom of that song or the advice from people around them have entered the system and have learned that lesson the hard way. Ironically, most of the people who have been convicted of a felony would not be considered hardened criminals. For the most part they are people who have made some bad decisions and are in desperate need of a second chance! Never-the-less; in this country an ex-felon will always be bond to and defined by the crime that they committed despite the fact that their debt to society has already been paid!

Should a person be punished for the rest of their life if they really don't deserve it? The answer is No! However; if you get convicted of a felony in the United States that's just what will happen, and whether you believe that this philosophy is right or wrong, the fact remains that both legal disability and social stigma are enforced against and attached to people with a criminal history: particularly those who have been convicted of a felony.

The politics of crime is responsible for creating an atmosphere of intolerance in this nation, and for over forty years politics have lubricated the machinery of the racially biased and thoroughly flawed criminal justice system that exists in this country today. Therefore; it goes without saying that politics have been the catalyst for the mass incarceration movement!

But that's just the tip of the iceberg! For hidden just beneath the surface of the political rhetoric are the sanctions that keep those who have a felony conviction imprisoned long after the sentence has been served. These sanctions stop you from getting a good job, a stable and safe place to live; they pull the social safety net out from under you, and brand you a social outcast once you have been released! The reason is that we live in a vindictive society, and the desire for vengeance has much more influence on the criminal justice system in the United States then the pursuit of true justice!

There is a punitive form of justice in this nation that belies the concept of what justice truly is. Unfortunately, it cannot give closure to the victim of a crime because it doesn't allow them to forgive nor does it provide an opportunity for redemption to the defendant because in America punishment is the sole and often disproportionate response to crime!

So let me ask you a serious question. How much is too much? I don't believe that you'll have the answer. On the other hand; neither do I! However; I now realize that the underlying reason why punishment in excess is accepted in America is the same reason that justice can't be served! The reason is that American's don't want true justice; they want the justice of revenge!

CHAPTER 1
VENGEANCE

It's the human emotion that wields the greatest influence on the US criminal justice system and the spiritual force that has taken control of this nation's war on crime and drugs. Bound in the hearts of a victim, their family and society; it will never allow them to forgive or forget. Placed into the hands of a jury; vindictiveness will undermine the presumption of innocence. When hidden in the mind of a prosecutor, it will over-charge the defendant, and disregard evidence that could exonerate, and when released from the mouth of a judge; it becomes the taskmaster that will enforce the punishment that's been handed down long after you're sentence has been completed!

It's the reason why our jails and prisons are overcrowded! It's solely responsible for the revolving door of recidivism stationed at the entrance of the Criminal Justice System, and it's the reason why a felony conviction haunts you for the rest of your life!

There is a very fine line between Justice and vengeance! That line is blurred when the force of human emotion hijacks the process of adjudication. When the method of judgment is not based in objectivity then justice will not be found. Moreover; where justice can't be found, there you will find hypocrisy and our criminal justice system is full of that. This is directly related to one of the strongest part of human emotion; the desire for revenge!

HYPOCRISY

Consider the fact that crime is pervasive in our society. Consider the fact that people of all races perpetrate crime virtually at the same rate and that people from the upper, middle, and lower classes are all represented. Consider the fact that you can break the law at any age, and that given the right circumstances anyone can be setting in the defendant's chair!

Taking everything into consideration you can see the hypocrisy in the system and within society as one is unwilling to forgive, the other is unable to forget and both fervently refuse to extend a second chance to those who have paid they're debt and have worked hard to earn it. I believe that the reason for this is that the spirit of vengeance understands that the desire for revenge is communicable! When its influence has been unleashed upon a community where a crime has been committed it will spread that desire like a virus and infect that community from one generation to the next! That's why most if not all defendants get more than they deserve and why everyone who has a felony conviction has to wear it like a scarlet letter for the rest of their lives!

Consequently, the scales that symbolize justice in this great nation are not filled with impartiality, integrity, and merit, based on the principle that the "punishment must fit the crime." Sadly; they are filled to the brim with fear, vindictiveness, and condemnation, based on the influence of a message that says; "once you're a criminal, you will always be a one." The fact that there are many ex-cons who have stopped breaking the law exposes that lie! With that said; why then have there been numerous laws and sanctions secretly enacted to punish convicted felons for the rest of their lives? I believe it's because of the power and the influence that the spirit of vengeance exerts on our lives changes the dynamics of interpersonal and societal relationships when a crime has been committed!

FORGIVEN, BUT NOT FORGOTTEN!

Now when you combine the power and the influence of the spirit of vengeance with human desire; it produces the propensity, and the propensity for vengeance creates in you a serious problem! That problem is called total recall! Over time it might let you forgive, but it will never ever let you forget! It gives the victim of a crime power over the defendant's future because not only does that propensity have an effect on the outcome of the trial, it also has an effect on the appeals process, on parole and probation decisions, and also on a convicted offenders chance to regain their civil rights once their debt to society has been paid!

The vast majority of criminal cases are victimless crimes however; when there is one, they don't want to know how truly sorry the defendant might be, or how determined they are to make amends. You see; an apology matters little to a grieving victim and their family because the propensity for revenge is driving them to seek only one thing! To see the perpetrator suffer like they did! And rightly so!

But how much is too much? Certainly no one deserves to become a victim of a crime. Conversely, the perpetrator of a crime deserves only what the law prescribes as punishment and no more; right? Wrong! That's never the case in the American criminal justice system because that propensity authorizes the spirit of vengeance to use a plethora of weapons that will keep the memory of what you did fresh in the minds of both the victim and society. From background checks and mug shot magazines to registration lists and public access to records, the spirit of vengeance has created too many roadblocks for a convicted felon to overcome. Makes no difference what you try to do to outlive your past, the long term memory that it creates in society limits your chances for a prosperous life long after your debt has been paid. It's the cloud that hovers over your head every day. It's a cloud in which there is no silver lining!

THE PERFECT STORM

Dark and foreboding; this is not just your ordinary rain cloud! It's called a super cell! It's a severe weather system that's filled with meso-cyclonic activity which is produced by two of vengeance's most violent hit men; Guilt and Shame! Now when the hot air of guilt converges with the cold air of shame, they twist themselves into a tornado so big that it will destroy everything in its path and leave in its wake very few survivors!

Beginning with the verdict, your guilt is declared by a so-called "jury of your peers," a panel of judges, or by entering a guilty plea yourself. Like a clap of thunder at the leading edge of the storm, your guilt sets off warning sirens alerting everyone that trouble is in the immediate vicinity. Lock your doors! Gather your family, and hide in your basement and sellers! Because a convicted felon is lurking or about to be released in your midst!

Now that's not bad advice to heed when inclement weather is bearing down on your location. It is even better advice when there is a habitual criminal that is being released in your neighborhood; even though they can and do change! However; the rumblings of what you did are not just directed at keeping that memory fresh in the mind of the victim and society, it's also a constant reminder to you of just how much of a loser you are!

LIGHTNING

Lightning flashing across the sky is a frightening yet awesome sight! The arcing of electricity exploding in the atmosphere can be more beautiful than fireworks on the fourth of July! But obviously; lightning is much more dangerous! In this ruthlessly engineered upper air disturbance, the spirit of vengeance uses shame as the power source for the lightning to inflict the deadliest part of its sinister plan! Why? Shame has the power to drive those who are not able to overcome the adversities that are apart of adjusting to life after incarceration back to prison or to take their own life!

Once you've been released from prison you will become a lightening rod in society. With pinpoint accuracy, bolts of shame strike your heart and set fire to your soul when the opportunities for advancement are blown away by the wind gusts that are fueling the turbulent atmosphere vengeance causes you to exist in. Darkness brings on depression, torrential rains drown out all hope, and a barrage of hail beats down upon your head to inflict wounds that you never seem to able to recover from. Sadly, in the wake of this perfect storm is the debris left behind from the shattered dreams and broken aspirations of a people who, (if they don't get set free), will have to spend the rest of their lives disconnected to and unaccepted by society! Buried alive in the grave clothes of disgrace, they will waste the seed of their God given potential in the desolate and unfruitful soil of a graveyard called mediocrity!

CHAPTER 2
CONSEQUENCES

Each decision that we make in life has consequences. Some are immediate and some are delayed. Some are short term and some are long term. Some help us to gain an advantage in life and some of them unfortunately are to our detriment. That's why it's so important for you to take head to wise counsel, consider all possibilities, and think before you act!

Unfortunately, that rarely happens when you're a child running the streets or you're a drug addict on a mission! When you're poor and hungry or you're rich and greedy! When you're desperate for love or you're driven by lust! When you're an envious "wannabee", or you're a self centered socialite!

Listen! Misery loves company! That's why it will always be the disappointed and downcast, the dysfunctional and disconnected, as well as the desperate and delusional that will do things that will cost them more than they are willing and are sometimes able to pay!

Now the consequences you will reap as a result of felony a conviction will be suffered in two phases. In the first phase there are the immediate consequences which will include the arrest, the conviction, the sentencing, and incarceration. In the second phase there are the delayed consequences which will include all the obstacles that you will have to face after reentering society. Without fail, the people that find themselves in this predicament only focus on the immediate because they have no idea that the delayed even exist.

THE IMMEDIATE

The immediate consequence of a felony conviction is the forfeiture of time. In addition, money is forfeited by the injunction of court ordered fines, restitution, and so called court costs, through criminal and civil cases at the local, state and federal levels. Included in this is the loss of personal income and Attorney fees. I am not opposed to convicted criminals having to serve time, pay fines, or restitution. I'm of the belief that wherever you make your bed is where you must lie! However, I have reservations about the amount of punishment that's being handed out. Why? It's because of the unjust sentencing policies! The unbridled discretion that prosecutors have in charging a defendant handcuff's judges at sentencing and is a central part of vengeance's sinister plan to take you out of society and keep you out for as long as it possibly can; whether you deserve it or not!

STRANGE BED FELLOWS

We live it seems in a society where going to the "joint" is a badge of honor. The fact that over two million people are locked up in state and federal prisons and local jails across this country might convince you that prison is the place to be. However, it isn't! Because when you make your bed in the darkness of a prison cell, you will never be prepared for the abusive relationship you will encounter with a cellmate named vengeance!

It has been said that "politics makes strange bedfellows." When this happens, it is by choice. An agreement made by two parties with different viewpoints that share a common goal. Consummated with a handshake behind closed doors it is the proverbial, "You scratch my back, and I'll scratch yours," scenario! It is consensual, calculated, and both sides stand to gain.

Not so with vengeance! For vengeance is a bully! It is not concerned with getting to know you. Nor is it looking for your consent. The only relationship it wants with you is the one in which it's in control. In this kind of relationship, the spirit of vengeance is the only one who stands to gain! That's because behind closed doors, it has devised a sinister plan to strangle the life from you spiritually, mentally, and ultimately physically!

Vengeance is a stalker! Its presence is felt immediately once you've been arrested and it invades your life upon sentencing. It plays with your mind and toys with your emotions until you arrive at the place of incarceration. Once you're in that cell and the doors slams shut, that is when the beat down begins!

With unfair treatment from prison staff, the unsanitary living conditions, the spread of STD's, TB, and other diseases, and the fear of spending time in a place called hell faced with life and death situations every day; this spirit has created an atmosphere in which there are only three ways to survive. #1 Fight; kill or be killed! #2 Surrender; be somebody's property or lay it down in PC! Or #3 Be assimilated; go in doing short time and end up doing life, or become a repeat offender that spends the rest of your life going in and out that revolving door!

Rape, gang violence, extortion of family members, latent and blatant homosexuality, set ups by inmates and/or prison guards, solitary confinement, racism, and the loss of personal property by theft or by shake downs. These are the horrors that you will have to confront in the place where the spirit of vengeance makes the rules and boldly declares; "This is my domain!"

Add to the pressure of trying to survive in the chaos of prison the burden that you are now carrying for the loved ones you have left behind. The victim is not just the only one who has had a crime perpetrated against them; it is also your family! Shunned by society because they are guilty by association, they also lose the income, (legal or illegal), that you provided. In many cases children are displaced by social services. Homelessness may become a harsh reality, and they are now defenseless to any retribution from the victim, their family, and their friends! Why! Because what you did placed your family directly in the cross hairs of a sharpshooter named vengeance!

THE DELAYED

When you plant a seed into the soil of criminality there are certain consequences that take time to grow! For the spirit of vengeance has built into its sinister plan road blocks, locked doors, trap doors, and barriers to hinder any progress you try to make once you have been released from its domain. The handcuffs and shackles, the chain linked fence, multiple rows of razor wire, and electronically locked doors that were used to confine you within the prison compound can't compare to the devices this spirit will use to keep you in its bondage upon your release.

There is something to say though about a person who endures the hardship of prison and comes out virtually unscathed. To do your time and come out with a purpose to live a better life is very admirable! However; having good intentions will not prepare you for the almost insurmountable odds that vengeance stacks up against you. For as soon as you hit the streets, your resolve will be thoroughly tested.

FAMILY

Some people have the love and support of family and friends to help ease the stress of life after incarceration. They can help them financially, help them find a job and give them a stable and safe place to live. Having that kind of moral support can shield them from the total impact of the delayed consequences and make them less traumatic! However, most ex-offenders do not have that in place! What's worse is that they did not have before they went in nor did they develop while they were in, the coping skills that would empower them to succeed in their endeavor to stay out!

Most of them get out with no place to go! Their spouses and significant others have left. Feeling angry and abandoned, they got with someone who could be there for them! In some cases this has provoked an, "If I can't have them, you can't either," response that has sent many people back to prison within days of their release!

If they are still there, winning their trust is always difficult! Yes they still love you but they resent you for what you did, and how what you did caused them to suffer! The children that never knew you or do not know you any more are hurting because they have had to endure a level of hardship no one should endure at such a young age! The worst thing is that they now are heading down the same path of destruction you did and are living under the curse that has been passed down through your family for several generations!

Now your words of wisdom hold no weight. In addition, your authority over them has been usurped by the sense of love and belonging they have received from the gang they represent! Maybe you are not allowed to see them at all for fear of the negative influence you might have on them regardless if you have changed or not! The destruction of the family unit is a tactical objective that the spirit of vengeance uses as a part of its arsenal of delayed consequences to tighten the strangle hold it has around your life!

EMPLOYMENT

In today's economy good jobs are hard to find. However; getting a minimum wage job is more difficult because of the social stigma that surrounds the hiring of an ex-felon! Any time you fill out a job application there is a good chance that you will be confronted with this question; "Have you _ever_ been convinced of a felony?" When that is on the application you are just wasting time because its automatic disqualification 99.99% of the time!

If you lie on the application, get the job, and the company finds out that you do have a felony, that will be grounds for immediate termination. If that conviction doesn't stop you from getting or keeping a job, it will stop you from getting a promotion, or put a ceiling on how high you can ascend that corporate later.

SOCIETY

When society discovers that you have a felony record you are looked upon differently. People will stop hanging out with you and you will become the topic of gossip at work and in your neighborhood. You'll be confronted with suspicion, treated with disdain, and if anything bad happens; you will be the first person they point the finger at! The amount of scorn and contempt that you encounter on a daily basis is vengeance's method of making you feel unaccepted in society! Castigated by an elitist mentality and relegated to second class status you have now become the scum of the earth!

The convicted felon is a pariah! Exiled and unwanted; among the categories of social outcasts they have been assigned the bottom rung of that ladder! The problem with that is that no one can tell who has been convicted of a felony without having direct access to inside knowledge. Unfortunately that knowledge has been made readily available on the internet! That proves that life is more challenging when you have a felony conviction than it is without one. So if you do have one; you need to know that the spirit of vengeance intends on making you suffer for it until the day you die.

But if you've paid your debt to society why do you still have to serve a life sentence? Is it fare for someone to get more than they deserve? If it is; then "justice served" is a lie! Justice requires, "an eye for an eye." But not vengeance! It demands your eye and much more! "Lock them up and throw away the key" if they deserve it is not enough. The only way to teach those who commit a crime and particularly a felony in this nation a lesson is to punish them and punish them severely! This proves that justice can never be served in America, because the spirit of vengeance can never be quenched!

CHAPTER 3
DISENFRANCHISEMENT AND COLLATERAL CONSEQUENCES

These are the laws and sanctions that most people in the United States, (let alone convicted felons), have little or no knowledge of! These punishments were enacted and are enforced because the spirit of vengeance has vision! While it cannot see what your purpose in life is; it can certainly see that you have a future! To keep you from finding and fulfilling that purpose, it has determined to use your past against you once you've reentered society!

So on the day you get released; it meets you at the prison gate, and with one hand it reaches back into the past. Grabbing a hold of your conviction it pulls it into the present; binding you to it and defining you by it. With the other hand it pushes your conviction along the pathway to the future; creating obstacles that are designed to keep you from achieving any success! Is there any wonder why so many have returned to a life of crime?

The spirit of vengeance has exceeded its quota by filling local jails and penitentiaries at the state a federal level with men and women doing their second, third, and fourth "bids!" Endowed with an infinite amount animosity; it skillfully uses the weapons of a corrupt legal system, a vindictive society, and the punitive nature of parole and probation to snatch away hope from the hearts of those who truly have changed and want to live a better life.

DISENFRANCHISEMENT

In general, disenfranchisement means to deprive a person of some or all of their civil rights! These laws are focused on stopping you from participating in the political process by revoking your right to vote based on a criminal conviction. These Felony Disenfranchisement laws are enforced in all fifty states and they vary in scope from one state to another.

The right to vote is a privilege that has been generally disregarded. We live in a nation that encourages its citizenship to take part in political process by choosing whom we want to lead us. However; voter turnout has been light. Numbers increase in presidential election years than in none, but for whatever reason, participation is not always what it should be! However, what if you wanted to vote and couldn't? What if you believed that your vote mattered and could make the difference in a hotly contested race, or a controversial issue but you were not permitted to do so? That's the dilemma a lot of ex-felons face when it's time to go to the polls and make our voices heard!

Depending on which state you reside in some have forfeited this right for the rest of their life! In some states you stay ineligible until you are released from prison, in others until parole or probation is completed. Some states require you to pay off your fines and restitution and catch up on your child support before you get reinstated, and in some states you have to go through a stringent process to prove that you deserve to regain that right!

Through much debate these laws have been modified but unfortunately they haven't been nullified! Why? Because vengeance will bend but it will not break! It knows that for anyone to be relevant in the future they must adapt to the changes that progress brings. So by systematically disqualifying ex-felons from participating in the political process overtime it will make them irrelevant. This has created a category people who are struggling to survive in a system that was designed to make sure that they fell.

CIVIL SERVICE

These laws apply when it comes to your constitutional right to serve as a state or locally elected official. As well as the right to serve jury duty! How ironic is that? Haven't we seen corrupt elected officials as well as corrupt jury members? The only difference between getting in trouble in the streets and getting in trouble in office is that the people in the street don't know who they are, and those in office have forgotten!

THE RIGHT TO BEAR ARMS

Your 2nd amendment right to bear arms can be denied if you are disenfranchised. Now I will agree that there are some ex-felons that should never be allowed to own a gun again! Conversely, there are some people who legally own fire arms that are felons waiting to happen! There is some irony in that, but isn't the purpose of the 2nd Amendment to insure your right to protect yourself, your family, and your property? And shouldn't regaining that right be based on more than just the fact that you committed a crime? Trying to justify my argument here is difficult since there is a correlation between crime and access to legal and illegal firearms. So I'll tread lightly here.

LIFE, LIBERTY, AND THE PURSUIT OF HAPPINESS

The Collateral Consequences of criminal convictions are secretly enacted sanctions that are invisible barriers set in place to disqualify you from certain jobs and careers and bar you from getting the licensing and bonding that are required to hold certain positions based on a felony conviction. They also disqualify those with felony drug convictions from acquiring government assistance as well. This means that they are not only disqualified from those careers, they are also denied the programs that were set in place to help people in need such as public housing, food stamps, student loans and grants based on a felony drug conviction!

This is very deceiving because the truth is, that it doesn't matter what kind of felony you have, it only matters that you have one and every public or private institution that employs, educates, or provides government assistance has the legal right to turn you away and slam the of doors opportunity in your face! Vision helps the spirit of vengeance skillfully wield this weapon of mass destruction to make sure that failure will be your only option.

The inalienable rights that were, "certain and held to be self evident," by our forefathers and that are recorded in the preamble of our constitution were envisioned by them to be extended to all citizens and protected by law. Nevertheless, if you have ever been convicted of a felony, you lose those rights and those rights in some cases can never be reinstated or reinstated only after a prescribed length of time when you have proved that you can live a crime free life and be a productive citizen once your prison sentence is completed.

The problem with that is that 2/3rd of the people being released from prison will be re-incarcerated within three years of their release. Why? Because vengeance will take away all of your constitutional rights through a process once called Civic Death long enough for you to decide that the only way to survive is to return to the things that got you in trouble in the first place! Its plan is for all the road blocks that you will encounter during the transition period between getting out of jail or prison and getting on your feet to discourage you and become the obstructive force that produces your destructive behavior. With the ultimate goal being to keep you off the streets for good by either putting you back behind bars or putting six feet under!

It's almost unfathomable, but this currant criminal justice system was never designed for rehabilitation! It was created to give the spirit of vengeance free reign and with this freedom it has placed limitations on the lives of those who have broken the law and establish a class of people who are oppressed by a multitude of covert sanctions making it virtually impossible to outlive their past! Currently there are over 5 million people in the United States that are disenfranchised and untold numbers affected by secretly enacted sanctions called Collateral Consequences of criminal actions! Most have already done their time and yet will still be serving time for the rest of their life because of what's been named the "invisible punishment!"

CHAPTER 4
MARKED

Singled out for surveillance, suspicion, hostility, an unpleasant fate; a marked man

The effect that vengeance has on the life of a convicted felon is far reaching. Forcing you to go through life burdened with trying to rise above almost insurmountable odds is its ultimate goal. Determined to break your will to succeed it will slam the doors of opportunity in your face, and trap you in a cyclical pattern of failure that proves to the world and to yourself that you are a marked man!

Ask someone that's been out of the joint for any amount of time, "How they're doing?" and if they're honest they would tell you that they're very glad to be out, but they've running from something they cannot describe, that's driving them in a direction they don't want to go!

Well my brothers and sisters that's not just your imagination! For the silhouette that appears in those reoccurring nightmares, that taunting laughter you hear every time the door of opportunity gets slammed in your face, that sinister presence you feel behind the resistance you have encountered as you try to rebuild your life, the footsteps echoing in the distance and the breath that you feel on the back of your neck; is from the relentless pursuit of an assassin named vengeance.

If they were honest! They would tell you that they have come to realize how difficult survival is when you're being chased down the road of infamy. For this is a cold, dark, and lonely existence in a world where the trio of torment; scrutiny, suspicion, and hostility are lying in wait for them around every corner.

The first contact that they had with this three headed monster made them realize that there are absolutely no advantages to being a marked man. Hiding your past is not an option because the spirit of vengeance provides many avenues of discovery to keep your conviction out in the open. On the other hand, if you are honest about what you've done, you can and will unintentionally invoke vengeance upon yourself. Finally you come to the realization that because of a felony conviction you have been singled out for an unpleasant fate.

FATE

With a felony conviction you have met the requirements for enrollment into the school of hard knocks. Unfortunately this is not an institution of higher learning. In spite of the fact that some poor souls brag that they have gotten their degree from this lowly place of academia, the type of knowledge you obtain here can only be prerequisite! This will allow vengeance to use its entire arsenal to suppress you making it virtually impossible for you to advance, graduate, and learn the true meaning of life by finding and fulfilling your purpose. Consequently; you learn to fake it, and not make it, to connive, and not strive. You will learn to deceive, not to conceive, to make an excuse, and not produce. You will learn not to live, only to survive, fear change and wallow in mediocrity. This is fate's recompense!

Fate, with all its twists is the diametric opposite of Destiny! It coexists in your life with Destiny, but what differentiates the two is the outcome. Fate will bring doom and gloom, Destiny will bring glory and honor! I believe everyone is born with a purpose. Finding and fulfilling your purpose in life will result in you completing your Destiny. On the other hand, if you miss or ignore that purpose your life will sadly have been a waste of time here on earth resulting from a string of bad decisions that ultimately sealed your fate! Destiny and fate fight hard for prominence in your life, and the decisions you make gives one or the other the authority to bring to fruition the seed bearing their predetermined ending. What's important to realize here is the fact that you will have a better opportunity to fulfill your destiny when vengeance is not a part of the equation.

Life is not lived on an equal playing field. The spirit of vengeance realizes that! But without an opportunity for manifestation its power is very limited. It can show off some of its power in the area of personal relationships. However, most relationship issues very rarely enter into the criminal justice system. But once you've been marked by the system because of a felony conviction, the chances to fulfill your destiny just became much more difficult. The setbacks that you suffer are strategically sent to impede and destroy your ability to make the right decisions. So with every disappointment, fate gains the initiative!

SCRUTINY

As a marked man all eyes will be upon you once you get released from prison. Even though you may dot every "I" and cross every "T", your motives will be questioned because everyone knows, "once you're a criminal, you will always be a criminal!" Everything you say and do will be judged against a standard that no one can uphold. That standard is enforced by the surveillance department of the Criminal Justice System known as the Adult Parole Authority and the Probation department.

At first glance these standards seem fare. They seem to be set in place to keep you from returning to prison. However, the true nature of Parole and Probation is punitive. Held over your head is the fact that you could be sent to or back to lock up at any time while under its supervision! It makes you feel like someone is pointing a loaded gun at your head that has no compunction about pulling the trigger! So by using surprise visits to your place of residence, your place of employment, and to your family and friends, the person who is charged with supervising your reentry seems to be searching for a reason to pull that trigger.

Sadly, a little thing like being late to a meeting could send you to or back to the joint! Not getting a job or a stable place to live even though the odds are stack against you or a negative report from those around you could send you to or back to lock up in a heartbeat! I'm not talking about a major infraction or a pattern of noncompliance. I'm talking about something as small as you not notifying your supervisor of the disagreement you had with someone, who in turn called him and made more out of it than what it really was to get you in trouble.

HOSTILITY

The hostility shown towards convicted felons is unprecedented. What will happen at places of employment and places of residency when your past has been revealed is a hostile campaign will be launched against you to get you fired or evicted. Vengeance uses the fear of what might happen, the ignorance of just what you did or did not do, as-well-as the rumors swarming around that ignorance, to ignite the fires of resentment towards certain types of felons, but all felons are included!

People have been attacked, property has been vandalized, lives have been threatened, and lies have been told. The hostility that is shown toward convicted felons is vengeance's way of telling them that it will not relent until the day you die. Defend yourself and you will be back behind bars before you can catch your breath. It matters not that you were the victim. It matters not that you've paid your debt to society. It only matters that the target that's been on your back since you were convicted gives anyone the right to try to take you out. Why? Because you've been tagged a felon by the system, branded an outcast by society, and singled out for destruction by the spirit of vengeance. You are a marked man and fate is trying to exercise its authority over your life by virtue of a series of bad decisions.

CHAPTER 5
VENGEANCE THE GREAT EMASCULATOR

Masculinity is under attack! Manliness is in the biggest fight of its life! The institution of manhood has been besieged on every side and from the cradle to the grave the image of what a man is supposed to be has been distorted! From soft and effeminate to hard and thuggish, the definition of manhood now includes these dysfunctional character traits! The first one is accepted as well as protected by law, and the second one is rejected and prosecuted by the law! However; both are targets of this punitive justice juggernaut.

Because of this; there is clearly a distinct disadvantage of being born male in the United States. Particularly a male of color! Since the declaration of the war on crime and drugs, vengeance has set out to weaken man's impact on the future of this nation using the criminal justice system as its primary weapon!

By surgically removing the man from his rightful place in society, vengeance has carved out a huge void in the fabric of America. Mass Incarceration has been the scalpel that it used to perform an operation that I referred to as, "Societal Castration!" The consequence of this procedure is that thousands of powerless men are being released into an unforgiving society! Sadly; this does not fill that void. What it does is it makes their manhood null and void!

Whether they are wasting time in prison being none productive or wasting time not able to be productive once they have been released; vengeance has been successful in it endeavors to weaken the man's impact on this nation's future by emasculating them through this new form of castration! Consequently, the people of this great country lift up their voices in unity with an outcry that will not be silenced until the void in the fabric has been filled.

EMASCULATION

The demand for men to step up to the plate of responsibility can be heard from every community in this nation. However; resonating the loudest have been the voices that emanate from the African American community! Why? Because with criminal intent vengeance has unleashed a weapon of mass destruction that has crippled it's psyche and rendered its men impotent.

Powerless; they strike out at the plate of responsibility. Cold; they have abandoned their children and have left their women unfulfilled. Wounded; they make no apology because they feel like they're owed one. Misunderstood; for outwardly they look like grown men however; inwardly they are little boys trying to get their Father's attention. Tragically their immaturity has enabled the spirit of vengeance to renew its claim to fame: which was and will always be the emasculation of the African American male, and enhanced it by adding the American male of all races!

We watched and done nothing as this syndrome invaded the "hood" and the barrios of America! Only when it encroached upon the suburbs and sub-divisions did we began to take notice! For vengeance unleashed a potent form of sterility that physically does not cause the inability to procreate; instead, like a virus it attaches itself to the spirit, injects its DNA, reproduces itself, and infects the male with a debilitating disease that causes vitiation; which is the inability to be effective.

In other words, this is a virus that attacks the very essence of manhood and obstructs the male's capacity to lead, to provide, to protect and deliver; resulting in a state of weakness, rebellion, and antisocial behavior. Once it's in the spiritual DNA, it can be transferred to his male offspring infecting one generation to the next! This is a condition that is pervasive in American society however; the biggest impact has been in the African American community!

Look! We all must realize that the spirit of vengeance cares nothing about the color of your skin, and that given the opportunity it can and will pounce on anyone. On the other hand, what we all must also come to realize is that this opportunistic disposition makes it solely responsible for the disturbing amount of racial disparity that prevails in the criminal justice system today! It's not that people of color commit crime at a higher rate than any other race; it's that they tend to do it in plain sight! For in the hood and barrio the corner office is outside on the street corner!

EMASCULATION BY INCARCERATION

This nation incarcerates over two million people! More than 35% of those locked up are African Americans. The problem with that is that they only represent 14 percent of the U.S. Population! The African American male has a 32% chance of being incarcerated at some point in life compared to Hispanics at 17% and Whites at 6%. The incarceration rate in 2009 of 748 in 100,000 was and is the highest in the world! In 2009 1 in every 10 African American men between the ages of 25-29 were locked up Compared to 1 in 28 Hispanic men and 1in 59 white men.

What does it say about America when it seems like a male is more likely to be sent to prison then to go to college, let alone graduate! What it's saying is that if we continue down this slippery slope we are headed for a great fall. However, it won't be an act of foreign terrorism that will bring this country to its knees. We will fall at the feet of the spirit of vengeance; an assassin that we have unleashed upon ourselves!

The warehousing of males in our jail's and prison's will prove to be the undoing of this nation simply because it is purely an act of retribution. In addition; the increase in crimes committed by boys that are under the age of 18 has presented vengeance ample opportunity to assault the institution of manhood. With brute force it severs the umbilical cord supplying the nourishment that turns boys into men, and it crushes the hopes and dreams of adolescence that are the building blocks for the foundation of manliness. Proving that the destruction of this country will be carried out by a domestic terrorist emasculating its men with a weapon called punitive justice!

EMASCULATED THEN ASSASSINATED

Capitol Punishment or the Death Penalty is the legalized lethal incapacitation of any person convicted of a capital crime. Is there not a better way to render a man ineffective than to kill him? Although I believe that there are crimes that warrant this punishment it does not change the fact that it is the perfect way to exact revenge. In fact it quenches the pallet of that blood thirsty tyrant.

Today there are 34 states that currently have death penalty statutes. That's including the federal and military statutes of the United States Government and Armed Forces. As of January 1, 2013 there were 3125 inmates on death row. 43% of them are White, 42% are Black, and 12% are Hispanic/Latino. Since the reinstatement of the death penalty in 1976 through May 1st, 2013 there have been 1330 executions.

On death row vengeance's onslaught far exceeds the level of torment that you would suffer while trying to maintain your freedom on the outside. Separated from the general population, the doom and the gloom you live under are exacerbated by the realization that you are among the walking dead. To sit in a 10x10 prison cell for 23 hours a day until your time comes to be strapped into a chair to be electrocuted or asphyxiated by poisonous gas, or to be strapped onto a gurney and given a lethal injection, or lead to the gallows for a noose to be put around your neck, or to stand before a firing squad, has to be unbearable! The closest thing to that most of us can identify with is being sent to our rooms by our Mother to wait for our Father to come home and give us our punishment! However, that is and there are no comparisons. Additionally, while you are wasting away in that cell for years, you are forced to watch as others go before you. You hold your breath as the guards lead him out in chains because you realize that's the fate that awaits you!

Your anxiety increases, your depression deepens, and insanity devours your mind. The nightmares of your impending death worsen each night, as each new day brings you closer to the date when the guards come for you. What makes it worse is that you could be rotting in that cell for 20 years! Unless an inmate fore goes the appeals process, they will maintain a slow rate of decomposition until the day of their impending death. Vitiated first by incarceration, then assassinated by the system with a method of your own choosing! No one should have to die that way, although some convicted felons truly deserve it!

Unfortunately, too many boys and men in this country have found themselves in this highly publicized yet unfavorable position. Since its reinstatement the death penalty has not been a deterrent to crime. But then; the spirit of vengeance never ever intended it to be! Its motive was never to slow crime down but to capitalize on the opportunity that crime brings to target and destroy the institution of manhood!

EMASCULATED STREET JUSTICE

The spirit of vengeance has a setting outside of the criminal justice system where it has been very successful. It's a place where ineffective boys and men have involuntary become the primary weapon of the Great Emasculator. It's a place where a person's life is worth less than another person's reputation. A place where being a thug is more honorable than being educated and gainfully employed. It's a place where females are referred to as, "bitch's and ho's," and who some say are more vicious than their male counter parts!

It's a place where the fate of little boys and girls is to carry on the family tradition of poverty, illiteracy, failure, addiction, violence and incarceration. It's a place where money and power are gained and maintained by violence! It's a place where the emasculated male carry's out his own kind of justice.

You can find that place in the streets of this nation! Where the graffiti found on the walls of buildings in the inner city is written in a new type of hieroglyphics; and when it is deciphered says, "Pay back is our way of life!" It can be found in the streets of suburbia where drunken fits of jealousy are retribution for marital infidelity and in the back roads of rural communities where street justice is still found at end of a rope or the barrel of a shotgun!

STREET JUSICE

Street justice is nothing new. It's in the streets of this nation where vengeance shines the brightest! Who needs a legal system when you can get revenge for yourself? It's in the streets where murder for hire is on the rise, and gang violence is at epidemic proportions. It's in the streets that disgruntled employees take out their frustrations on their supervisors and co-workers. It's in the streets where we see school shootings carried out by kids who were provoked by bullies. It's in the streets where mass murder is becoming common place. It's in the streets where, "payback is a mutha"!

It used to be, "If you take mine I'll take yours!" Now it's, "Take mine and I'll kill you and yours!" This form of street justice is a by any means necessary, no holds barred, take no hostages, leaves no witness's, get them before they get you, kind of justice. The emasculated male perpetrates over 80% of the bloodshed in the streets of America, and like an executive producer the spirit of vengeance has written, edited, choreographed and directed a tragically gruesome reality series that pits male against male. The worst thing about this is that they don't even realize that they have the leading roles in a horror story that ends like this, one will die, and one will go to prison for the rest of his life! Ironically; the ineffective male has been very effective in destroying themselves, as-well-as this entire nation no thanks to vengeance, the "Great Emasculator"

CHAPTER 6
VENGEANCE AND THE MEDIA

For well over forty years the media has been the spirit of vengeance's greatest asset. This multifaceted outlet has become the pulpit from which it can preach its fearful message to the masses. Like a vaccination, it immunizes society with an antibody that makes the people resistant to the principle of the presumption of innocence, and also to the fact that a convicted felon can truly change.

Its message can be heard from the cable news network to the local and national news programs. Its message can be heard from the specialized programs and investigative reports to the daily news paper and gossip magazines. From talking heads on television and radio talk shows, to Twitter, Face book, My space, the blogs, chat rooms, and You tube, vengeance has fashioned this 21st century technology into a wet stone that sharpens the blade of the weapon it has used against all humanity for many thousands of years and the name of that weapon is character assassination!

THE SWORD AND POLITICS

Vengeance thrives in the campaign of a savvy politician who makes his platform the war on crime and drugs. Using the media he plays on society's fear of becoming a victim. Reminding the people that drugs and alcohol are destroying their neighborhoods, gangs are kidnapping and brainwashing their children, automatic weapons are easily obtained by the criminal element and the streets outside their homes are not safe for little children to play in. He adds to his constituency daily by reiterating the reasons for the troubles in this nation. Vowing to clean up the mess, he makes a promise that if he's elected to pass stricter laws, hand out harsher sentences, build more prisons, and keep those who commit crimes off the streets for good.

This platform successfully launched the careers of many elected officials. On the other hand, it has also destroyed the careers of many of the same! Why? It's because a fancy suit and a charismatic personality will not stop the media onslaught when that official is hit by scandal. You see, vengeance will allow you to stand on its platform and peddle its influence through the media, but at the same time; it will use the media to expose your hypocrisy then crush you beneath the weight of that very same platform.

Recently we have seen several political careers destroyed by the spirit of vengeance because of hypocrisy, but their platform was different. Their platform was Family values. Sometimes power goes to the head of these people and they forget about upholding the honor of the office they were elected to, or they simply think they are above reproach because of that office. Whatever the reason is, it is an open invitation for vengeance through the media to do its thing.

Some top officials leap on the vengeful bandwagon as soon as a colleague's infidelity is exposed. Boisterously leading in the rhetoric calling for their colleague to step down until their own infidelity is exposed by the media. Some profess their conviction in the belief that the definition of marriage is the union between a man and a woman and that homosexuality is not an alternative lifestyle. They spearhead the campaign against same sex marriage, until the media exposes their true sexual identity. The sordid array of immoral conduct ranges from visiting prostitutes to child pornography. From secret affairs, to the revelation of illegitimate children; all of these things are huge factors that contribute to the destruction of the family unit!

If the platform is fiscal responsibility, the spirit of vengeance will find a thief. If it is race relations, it will expose a bigot. If it is the war on terror, it will uncover a cover up. If it is national security, it will identify a traitor. The relentless pursuit of a story that can be tried in the court of public opinion will not let the media rest. For it is their job to bring to light the wrong doings of those we have entrusted to represent us in the matters of this nation. That's what vengeance wants them to believe so longs as someone looses their job, family, influence, and reputation. It matters not if what is said about them is the truth or a lie; once the sword of character assignation is done carving you up it will be virtually impossible to get full restoration. Let alone getting the process started at all.

WORDS CREATE ATMOSPHERE

If people understood that the purpose of the spoken word is not just to communicate but to create and maintain the atmosphere in which they live in, we would be much more careful about what we say and how we say it. Taking advantage of people's ignorance of this principle, the spirit of vengeance capitalizes on the emotionally charged words used by both the victim and society to create and maintain an atmosphere for punitive justice!

In today's criminal justice system Press Conferences have been an invaluable tool used by the spirit of vengeance to invert principle of the presumption of innocence. For in the court of public opinion emotions prevail, and when emotions prevail, the words that are spoken create and maintain an atmosphere where the opposite is true, you are "guilty until proven innocent."

Perched on the steps of the court houses all across this country with cameras rolling are city officials who use words to paint a picture for the public of the monster they are looking for or that they have in custody. Prosecuting

Attorneys use carefully chosen words so as not to reveal their case and simultaneously stir up the atmosphere promising that the defendant will be prosecuted to fullest extent of the law. That combined with the emotionally charged statements from the victim and their families will provoke a level of community outcry for revenge that is so high the defense attorneys have to ask for a new venue because the media coverage has infected the jury pool in that community with a lethal dose of, "I'm gonna get you sucker!"

The bright spectacle of televised criminal proceedings has become a permanent fixture in this nation's criminal justice system. Cameras in the court room give us a bird's eye view of how the system really works, at the same time creating and maintaining America's insatiable appetite for revenge.

The programs that are on cable channels like Court TV all have commentary coming from a so called expert panel of mostly hot heads, that spew vengeful words to create the type of environment conducive for viewers to call in from places that are not in the same jurisdiction of the trial so that they can vent their frustrations, pass judgment or condemn the defendant, and make snide remarks on a trial that they have nothing to do with. In other words, it gives society and opportunity to cast the first stone or get their pound of flesh.

TALK SHOWS

Talk shows have been the bastion for emotionally charged words and opinionated conversation. They are the Petri dish where vengeance's growth is unhindered. Under the 1ST amendment the spirit of vengeance knows that it's diatribes from these shows are safe in the hands of our founding fathers. On issues ranging from abortion to the death penalty the hosts of these shows engage in verbal warfare with the pundits for and against each topic. Like arsonists they start forest fires that burn uncontrollably, they reinforce walls of division in this country, and are a huge factor that is contributing to its eventual down fall.

GLAMORIZING REVENGE

The movie industry has cashed in on our unquenchable thirst and undeniable addiction to the spirit of vengeance. Tens of millions of dollars are spent by production companies in the making of a movie to rake in the hundreds of millions of dollars that are received at the box office from movie goers around the world. Why? Because vengeance is a crowd pleaser! It satisfies the need for retribution through the characters of each film, and has inspired many perpetrators to commit the gruesome acts of retaliation they've seen in the movie!

The spirit of vengeance has a star on the Hollywood walk of fame. Glitz and glamour, fame, fortune, and the lifestyle of the rich and famous have been its reward. For the media's depiction of vigilantes, gangsters, thugs, and good folks gone bad has made revenge more popular than forgiveness, and more accepting than giving people a second chance.

Probably the most effective use of the media by the spirit of vengeance is the music videos of the Hip Hop genre. Romanticizing gangs and the vicious way they handle their business has made a deep, dark and destructive impression on this generation. The mantra that is repeated in each and every video and song has created an atmosphere were vengeance is celebrated in this country. They party all night long and embrace the fact that if they live by the sword, they're going to die by it! Without hesitation these kids are ready to kill someone over something as small as a disrespectful look and are willing to die for the gang that they represent! Sadly; these "gangstas" have no respect for life; not even their own!

THE SWORD IN SPECIAL PROGRAMING

As I write this part of the book I almost feel like apologizing. Why? Because it seems like that I am about to exact vengeance on an American icon and that's not my intention! However; exposing the depth that the spirit of vengeance will go to express itself has a funny way of making good intentions look bad.

The special programs I am talking about focuses on catching criminals that are on the run. There is no doubt that they need to be caught and locked up so that they cannot harm anyone else. However; while they provide a needed service in helping to capture wanted fugitives, these shows serve as conduits for the victim and society's desire for revenge! Even so; if anyone needs an advocate it is surely the victim of a crime. Someone that they can put their confidence in to help them get the closure that they need, not just in word but also indeed! Someone who has stood in their shoes, has cried the same tears, and felt the same pain. Someone who has suffered a great loss and who has grieved just like they did.

We have found that in Adam Walsh and Americas Most Wanted. For over 25 years he, his foundation, and his ground breaking TV program have fought relentlessly for victims rights, were instrumental creating and getting pass the Adam Walsh Child Protection and Safety Act, helped in the capture of 1100 of America's most dangerous fugitives, as well as help bring home 65 missing children.

Energized by his own personal tragedy, he and his wife co-founded an organization called the National Center for Missing and Exploited Children, and has led the charge for legislation to protect against child predators. Through his foundation and hit television series, he has made all of America a safer place to live. For that we owe him a huge debt of gratitude. However, vengeance plays a huge part in all that has been accomplished.

But that's what the victim and society want; the justice of revenge! Yet sadly closure for them will not come when vengeance is exacted. Once the sentence is pronounced the finality of the experience is short-lived. The proof of that is in victim's statements! The prevailing theme of those statements seems to always be hate, unforgiveness, and the desire to see their perpetrator suffer. Any amount of time that is given is never enough, because it will not relieve the pain, and sadly; unhealed wounds won't let you forgive, and you cannot find closure if there is no forgiveness. That's why a person needs more than just a band aid placed over the gaping wound they received as the result of being victimized!

So what is hidden in the midst of the advocacy and hidden in the midst of all the hard work is the same thing that can be found concealed in the capture, the conviction, and the sentencing. That thing is retribution. It is the driving force behind everything and the reason for all the success. How sad is it that the good that has come from all this effort can be attributed to the spirit of vengeance and its use of the media.

CHAPTER 7
MENTAL BEAT DOWN

If you think you can't, you won't even try! This is the mentality that the spirit of vengeance strives to indoctrinate a convicted felon with to enlist and maintain membership in the fraternity of the emasculated male. Even if you desire to forget the past and pursue a new life, all the disappointments that you will face have the power to change that desire into hopelessness. The weight of hopelessness will through attrition crush your dreams of living a successful life; leaving you cold and calloused, demoralized and defeated. Understanding that quitters never prosper, its purpose is to make you quit even before you get started.

It will start off subtly, and then blatantly attack the mind of a convicted felon trying to get off the road to infamy. With a combination of real and perceived discrimination, the laws that limit your successful reentry, and a severe case of low self-esteem the spirit of vengeance attacks your mind and forces you into mental instability! Consequently, the depression that you live under is much darker since vengeance is the one who is concealing the light, and the anxiety that's overwhelming you is much more terrifying because vengeance has taken on the form of the intimidator. What is its ultimate goal? To diminish your capacity to adjust to life after prison by driving you completely out of your mind!

"FIT IN" OR "GIVE IN"

The heat is on and the pressure is at the boiling point when you exit the confinement of a penal institution to reenter an unforgiving society. The irony is that while you do not know what to expect once you get out, you do realize that the odds are stacked against you. In this case, what you don't know is definitely what's going to hurt you because that lack of knowledge is exactly what gives vengeance the initiative and allows it to maneuver you into situations where the consequence of each decision you make results in utter failure!

The spirit of vengeance has sold you a bill of goods called rehabilitation. This refers to the state provided programs that ultimately turn out to be a waste of your time and the tax payer's money since it's highly unlikely that you will get the chance to use them because of the stigma that attaches itself to ex-offenders! So if you really want to know the truth; it's all a big set up!

As a convicted felon you've been setup to believe that society is willing to give you a second chance. You have been tricked into thinking that by getting your G. E. D. or earning a degree you will be able to find a good job. You were deceived by the promise that if you are remorseful for what you did, you will find forgiveness. Finally, you've been mislead by the erroneous belief that once your sentence is completed and you have paid your debt to society, there is no more obligation and no strings attached. By the time you realize that you've been lied to, you just might be in the midst of a nervous breakdown.

The road to redemption is a tough one to stay on! Since your goal can only be achieved through perseverance and the systems method of exacting revenge is slow and deliberate, somehow you must find a way to prevail in this battle of attrition! What you will quickly find out however, is that this is very difficult; for persistence is vengeance's claim to fame!

Its strategy is to wax triumphantly in this war by slowly and deliberately eliminating all of your options; then make you choose from the alternatives it gives you! You will have to determine whether to "fit in" or to "give in!" Unfortunately, whichever one you choose to do will signal your submission to the mental and emotional torment that has destroyed the lives of so many and has at the very least kept them locked behind the bars of a psychological jail cell.

"FIT IN"

The definition of "fit in" is to become something you are not. For that to happen, vengeance has to convince you that the only way to survive in a society where there is no such thing as a second chance for those who have been convicted of a felony is to live a lie, and to hide what you did through art of deception. Now the spirit of vengeance is the ultimate liar; and unbeknownst to you it will use the power of suggestion to help you deceive most of the people who do not know the real you, and some of people who really do! However, its true motive is to make you believe your own lie.

Self deception is the ultimate form of self denial. For denying self expression, which includes both "the thrill of victory and the agony of defeat," only puts constraints on your chances of achieving success after you have been incarcerated. Why? Because the "can of whip ass" that vengeance breaks open on your mind keeps you focused on hiding what you did, instead of on moving away from what you did in an attempt to stave off the tremendous amount of social and political opposition you have and will continue to face because of your conviction. Additionally, when you deny that part of your past, vengeance sets you up for a fall and then waits for the right opportunity to expose you for the liar that you really are! Now the other side of this is worth repeating. If you talk about that part of your life, you can and will invoke vengeance upon yourself. So when it's all said and done, you can't win for loosing. You are caught between a rock and a hard place, and that's exactly where it wants you to be.

"GIVE IN"

"Give in" means: to forfeit the initiative, relinquish authority, hand over the prerogative, and admit defeat. It is unconditional surrender. This is the decision that vengeance intends on forcing you to make because it has an easier time holding you down when you are unable to or unwilling to fight back. Capitulation will qualify you for a life time membership in an organization it founded many years ago called the "Association of Emasculated Men", aka, "Club Loser"! With chapters in every village, township, city, and county in all fifty states, it's the biggest fraternity in America!

As member of this association, a loser is entitled to multiple all expense paid trips to be locked up at the local jail or the state and federal penitentiary. To be disowned by family and friends and scorned by society. To be re-addicted by the drug of choice that ultimately contributed to their initial down fall, and to be victimized by an open form of discrimination that the law upholds and promotes. All of that comes along with the mental abused that in many cases has caused a convicted felon to take their own life or worse yet; cause them to exploded and take someone else's!

So when you look at the alternatives that vengeance forces you to choose from, you really have no choice at all. However, when you live on the verge of a mental breakdown you'll do anything to get relief. Unfortunately, there is no relief when you have submitted to the will of the spirit of vengeance. The only thing that is left to do is accept the beat down because there is no fight left in you!

THE BEAST

There is a menace to society that society is not prepared for! Created by a preemptive strike that was called the "get tough on crime" movement; vengeance has wasted more minds then drugs and alcohol combined. The mental instability that a convicted felon enters society with will be exacerbated by the will to survive. This can and has caused them to be more of a threat to society then they were before they went in.

The monster that now walks the street is one step away from a psychotic episode. Why, because the spirit of vengeance has concocted an elixir that is made up of two bitter tasting toxins called disappointment and failure, and mixed it with the sweet taste of freedom. Once it's ingested the poison attacks their mind and releases a fear so intense that it brings out the worst in them.

Using instinct over intellect, the creature circumnavigates the everyday challenges that vengeance confronts him with, in the attempt to make life after incarceration a little bit easier to deal with. They walk out of prison knowing that they don't have what it takes to stay on the outside, so they'll do what they have to do to keep their freedom as long as they can, vowing that they'd rather die than to be lock up again!

Now the beast that roams the streets is looking for an excuse to explode. One more disappointment could send him over the edge. One more failure could make him fly off the handle. One more door slammed in his face could be the straw that breaks the camel's back. One more tear falling from the eyes of his wife or significant other because they don't know how the families going to make it could be what trigger's the explosion that causes him to take his frustrations out on society, or the next person he comes in contact with! Just one more thing!

Society's propensity for payback that has unleashed the spirit of vengeance and allowed it to wreak havoc with the American criminal justice system unrestrained has resulted in the opposite effect of what it was intended to do. The intent was to make this nation a safer place to live in, to be a deterrent, and to play a part in the rehabilitation of those who break the law. Sadly, with vengeance at the helm, instead of being a deterrent, the crime rate increased! Instead of feeling safer, we became more fearful than ever before, and instead of rehabilitating criminals, it has manufactured a better one! No, society is not prepared for the beast that was created by the "get tough on crime movement"! The scary thing about this is that the beast is now either already walking the streets of your community, or it's just about to be released!

Over 600,000 of these convicted felons are being released on the door steps of our communities all across the country every year! What's ironic is that we've created a beast and do not know how to tame it! The worst thing is that this nation has not yet learned the lessons that come from being a vindictive society.

CHAPTER 8
THE ABDUCTION
OF LADY JUSTICE

For well over four decades the prevailing viewpoint on how justice is administrated in this great nation has been defined by a series of laws and policies whose name has become the battle cry of a society that is intoxicated on the spirit of vengeance. The "Get Tough on Crime" movement was and is made up of a set of policies that truly exemplify the punitive and vindictive nature of human emotion, and simultaneously identifies itself as being solely responsible for its own failure.

Its purpose was never to serve as a deterrent or to function as an instrument of rehabilitation. Its purpose was to punish and to punish severely! With that in mind, the spirit of vengeance secretly high jacked the seat at the bench of adjudication in the American criminal justice system and placed an imposter who looked like Lady Justice to doled out a form of justice that was intended to cut deep and leave lasting scares on those who break the law like the lash of a whip does on bare skin. This resulted in the marginalization of millions people, and skyrocketing rates of incarceration and recidivism!

The "tough on crime" movement refers to policies that emphasize punishment as the primary, and often sole, response to crime. Mandatory sentencing, Three strikes, truth-in-sentencing, zero tolerance, and various other proposals that result in longer and harsher penalties and that eliminate rehabilitation and other programs are all contemporary examples of "tough on crime" policies.

But do these policies really reflect the true nature of Justice? Because if there's an imposter seated at the bench of adjudication, does it not stand to reason that true Justice cannot be administered nor can it's true nature be reflected. Although crime must be punished, in a system where punishment is its primary response, vengeance exploits the rightness of punishment by creating an atmosphere of fear and intolerance. This atmosphere has made it conducive for targeting the biggest perceived threat against American society. Which was, and is today, the rise in criminal activity.

Targeting the rise in criminal activity is not the problem! There has to be laws enacted as well as policies set in place to keep our neighborhoods safe and to punish those who break them. The problem is that because of the "get tough on crime" initiatives the spirit of vengeance was able to kidnapped Lady Justice and changed the focus of the Criminal Justice system from enforcing the law to oppressing a people! This resulted in what we can call the biggest policy failure that the world has ever seen.

Fortunately the voices that opposed this movement for years have recently made some inroads in bringing about changes in these policies. We've learned that through attrition that vengeance will bend, but it will not brake. The reason for this I believe is that no one realized that Lady Justice had been abducted. Ironically; this is not due to the fact that the imposter has played her to the "t", it is due to the fact that the more you drink the prettier that ugly girl gets! You see; we thought we went home with the beauty, but instead we woke up with the beast. Since the mid 1960's our society has been inebriated on vengeance, and all we have to show for it at this point, is what seems to be an incurable hangover.

FEAR AND INTOLERENCE

The abduction was stealthy. For it came at a time in our country's history when social upheaval was at a peek and the proponents of change were kicking down barriers faster than the opponents of change could rebuild them. That's when vengeance high jacked the system with a punitive doctrine that would eventually persuaded even the proponents of change that the current laws were soft on criminals, and placed a charlatan in the seat of adjudication!

Declaring war on crime, it shifted this nation's focus from social welfare to social control. In other words, instead identifying the root causes that contribute to the upward spike in criminal activity and addressing them, this pretender utilized phrases like, "crime in the streets," as-well-as "the breakdown of law and order," to take away the distinction between civil disobedience and public disturbance and collectively criminalized both responses to the opponents of change's desire to maintain the status quo.

This "tough on crime rhetoric" establish an atmosphere of intolerance, which then gave the imposter a platform to call for and enforce social control policies through swift and severe punishment. Whether it was a violent riot in the north or a peaceful non-violent protest in the south, no one was exempt! However this is not the true nature of Justice!

A HAMMER NOT A GAVEL

It is oppression at its best! Or should I say at its worst! It is vengeance in full force. For this imposter wields a hammer not a gavel to pound on the heads of those that it feels intimidated by the most. In a system driven by conservative politics, the hammer is the most effective way to administer social control to ensure that they have an electoral advantage over their liberal counter parts. Eventually, this would become bipartisan politics, when the liberals got in line and took up the hammer to try to gain this advantage.

The politics of social control has been very expensive. The platform that this hammer has built has cost this country more than just the total amount of money already spent on this failed attempt at maintaining the status quo. I'm referring to the abduction of Lady Justice and the fact that there has not been a request for ransom. Truthfully; this imposter understands that it has lost the war on crime and drugs a long time ago, yet it still bides its time in the seat of adjudication at the behest of a society that remains under its influence!

Over forty years ago a secrete overthrow of the Criminal Justice System allowed an imposter to exact vengeance unrestrained. It and it alone has been solely responsible for the upward spike in recidivism, the emasculation of the American male, and the breakdown of the fabric of this nation. Crime has not been deterred; and often times the punishment does not fit the crime. To date this nation has the highest incarceration rate in the world, and with over two million people locked up there seems to be no end in sight!

But where is Lady Justice now? Has she just given up without a fight? No! She is fighting behind the scenes; for she took a vow a long time ago to never give up on this nation. Although overshadowed by the presence of this imposter; I have seen her at work in the midst of its tenure. I have seen her free those that have become victims of vengeance! Yet she can only do so much because like an alcoholic our society has an addiction to the spirit of revenge! But the time has come for her to be freed! When Lady Justice takes back her seat at the bench of adjudication we will be able to successfully win this war. Because the only way that Justice can be served in this nation is for her to break the mental addiction that this society has to vengeance.

CHAPTER 9
THE BODY OF JUSTICE

If you were to evaluate someone for a new job, a promotion, or a certificate of merit, you would look at that person's body of work. You would take into consideration things like the contributions that they've made to their community, their successes and failures, their leadership skills and their ability to mentor. You would try to find what distinguishes them from the other candidates and what makes them qualified for this important position or prestigious award you have to offer.

In a day in which integrity is an attribute that is hard to come by, it is imperative for us to find the right person for the opportunity at hand. For the evidence is clear; if the wrong person gets into a position of influence their failure will bring shame to the institution they represent, dishonor to the office that they hold, or quite possibly take down and entire nation.

WANT ADS

The state of employment in this country is now on the rise. One thing that we do know for sure is that hard times do not come to stay, they come to pass. Based on that statement, it is my opinion that we will rebound from this economic crisis and in turn cause the world's economy to rebound as well. Until then jobs, especially good jobs will stay in great demand. Nevertheless, there is a job opportunity that those who still believe in this great nation are offering and it needs to be filled immediately. That opportunity is to fill the seat at the bench of adjudication and oversee this nation's entire criminal justice system.

Although occupied by an imposter, the position that we have to offer has been vacant for over four decades. What we are seeking is an entity that truly personifies the very essence of American society! One who is made up of a substance that is rich in integrity and is steeped in the belief that justice is for all! One who is motivated by the passionate pursuit of true justice, and who understands that this is only achieved by the solemn practice of objective and impartial adjudication! One who has paid the price for loyalty! However, its loyalty is not for sale! One who's devotion is to uphold and enforce the laws that govern this nation, to protect its people, as well as to administer true justice equally.

What we are seeking is an entity whose voice can permeate society and break the mind set of fear that was exacerbated by the get tough on crime rhetoric of old and create a new mindset that gives our society the courage to take punishment from being the sole and often disproportionate response to crime, and make the punishment fit, bring closure to the victim, and address the causes of crime and recidivism to make those rates decrease and keep them on a down ward spiral. What we are seeking is an entity that has empathy for the victim however; is not moved by the torrent of emotions that is stirred up by desire for revenge. Whose judgment may not quench the blood thirstiness of that tyrant but will satisfies the requirements that the law prescribes for justice to be served.

THE HEAD

There is one entity that can fulfill all the prerequisites that we require for the job being offered. Only one entity has truly distinguished itself! Rising to the top of all other applicants, it has proven itself uniquely qualified to be awarded this prominent position! There is only one, and that entity is Lady Justice, and her body is the testimony of the work that she has performed and will perform again!

In our evaluation of Lady Justice we see that her head is enshrouded in a blindfold. This is one of the unique qualities that make her standout from all the other applicants. You see, if rightness is to prevail in the criminal justice system then he who sits in the judgment seat must be blind. This imposter is predisposed to corruption due to its unobstructed view of the world. On the other hand, the blindfold that she wears represents strong moral values.

Impartiality can only be administered if there is no place in the system for corruption! Corruption cannot have a place in the system if the one who is seated at the bench of adjudication has strong moral values. Strong moral values will override the propensity for vengeance even in the face of the most heinous crime! Strong moral values resist temptation when money tries to change hands. Strong moral values are the great equalizer when race looks for privilege or bigotry tries to maintain the upper hand! With strong moral values Lady Justice will make sure that the judicial process results in an outcome that makes both the victim and perpetrator agree that justice has been served whether they like it or not!

THE HANDS

As we further evaluate Lady Justice, we are fascinated by what she holds in here hands. Just as the imposter uses a plethora of weapons to exacted revenge, so too does Lady Justice! However, she has the advantage because she needs fewer weapons to administer justice!

She will take the seat at the bench of adjudication equipped with a two fisted attack that is powerful enough to deter crime, protect society, and punish law breakers. In one hand she wields a double edged sword, and in the other she holds a scale. But the impact of each weapon is not as effective individually as they are combined. Now the double edged sword represents her authority to enforce the law and to punish those who would break it. The scales represent her ability to objectively apply the law based on the merit of each case.

That being said, we now understand that the failure of this current system is the use and abuse of the swords impact. With the outcry for vengeance and the enactment of the "get tough policies," the sword has no restraint. It cuts and slices at the fabric of America with reckless abandon. It plunges its blade to the hilt in every case, even if it is not warranted. The reason is that the imposter has replaced objectivity with subjectivity, and has allowed human emotion to take precedence over merit.

Not so with Lady Justice! She wields the sword to protect and punish by enforcing the law in fairness and equality. Each case is weighed in a balance to ensure that society feels her blanket of protection and that the appropriate amount of punishment is handed down. When the punishment fits the crime, the rightness of that punishment cannot be argued against. This gives Lady Justice the authority to provide closure to the victim.

THE FEET

The final part of the evaluation of Lady Justice is to consider her ability to stand! She has proven that she will up hold the standard of rightness by treating both the victim and the offender with impartiality. For she understands that the law demands that those who sit at the seat of adjudication must insure that they do not turn the victim into a perpetrator and that the law doesn't make the perpetrator its victim.

The ability to stand up for others is an inherent trait that is called advocacy. It is the fundamental element needed for justice to be served. We all know that the dual purpose of the law is to protect and to punish. However, we all need to understand that the security promised to us from the law is grounded in the belief that justice is for all and that justice cannot be enticed!

This is the reason why she stands with one foot firmly planted on the book of the law symbolizing that the rule of law is not subject to personal interpretation but subjects all of us to personal and corporate obedience, and with the other foot firmly planted on the head of a snake to symbolize that the one who sits in the seat must not be subject to temptation but have the power to overcome it!

That cannot be said about this imposter, because she is a whore! She continues to sell her personal interpretation of the rule of law to anyone for the right price. Unfortunately this has infected the legal system with a malignant form of cancer that can only be treated with her being removed from the system. In other words, criminal justice in this country needs a "system-ectomy!"

But the greatness of Lady Justice is the foundation on which she stands! It's the strong and enduring foundation that was laid to build this great country of ours on. That foundation is that "all men are created equal". Throughout the years she has stood up against racial inequality! She has stood up for civil rights! She has stood up for the poor and defenseless, and she has stood up against injustice of all kind. She has stood up on that foundation and looked into the face of the spirit of vengeance and cried with a loud voice; "Justice must be and will be served!"

Made up of the material needed to patch the hole in the fabric of this nation, she's the only entity for the job. She breathes equality; which is the essence needed to resurrect this dead and broken system. The rightness that flows from her spirit will have the authority to break society's addiction to vengeance! She is exactly what we need! She is Lady Justice

CHAPTER 10
LAWS FOR JUST US

"If you're looking for justice, that's just what you'll find — just us."

Richard Pryor

For justice to be served there has to be a set of standards in place that are recognized by the people as binding and are enforceable by those in authority. In other words there must be laws. A set of rules and regulations that define what will not be tolerated, or accepted, that are considered by both the people and those who are in authority if they are broken as a crime. In addition, these laws are put in place in order to protect those who abide by them, to punish those who break them, as well as be a deterrent to those who would contemplate perpetration. Without them there would be anarchy!

History shows that a set of laws have always been establish to govern cities, states, and nations as far back as the reign of the Sumerian King Urukagina, who ruled the city state Lagash in Mesopotamia from 2380BC-2360BC. His statutes are considered the first example of legal reforms in recorded history.

More recognizable to most of us is the code of King Hammurabi, who ruled the Babylonian empire from 1792BC-1750BC. From that time until now, there is and will always be laws set in place to make certain that justice can be served. But laws can create problems. What we as nation have experienced serves as an example of how the law can be used to oppress the people.

The problem that we have in the United States is not the concept of having laws, it is the impact of the laws that those who are in authority have conceived! For at least the last four decades those who are in authority have been more concerned with pushing their own agenda than being focused on the concerns of the people that they represent. Consequently, laws that are supposed to be set in place to protect, deter, and punish became instruments used for targeting, control, and harassment.

It is the nature of mankind to respond to victimization by seeking revenge. Not only is it a natural response, it's an emotional one as well. Taking advantage of that emotion, those who are in and have been in authority have reshaped the concept of Justice in this nation by implementing the policies of the Social Control Agenda. This agenda has a target and that target has become the victim of inequality in this nation's criminal justice system. This is proof that the laws they conceive are unjust.

If you haven't realized it by now, Let me help you understand the fact that we live in a nation where the specter of inequality looms large. That means the void between the haves and the have not's is widening. What you need to know is that fame and fortune, power and prestige, position and popularity will gain you access to places where those who don't have these luxuries are denied! In no other place is this more evident in this country than in the criminal justice system.

That's where the more money you have, the more likely it is that you will get away with what you've done, or at the very least not go to prison. Additionally, where the color of your skin makes you more or less likely to be stopped, arrested, convicted, incarcerated and disenfranchised, whether you're guilty or not.

LAWS FOR JUST US

"[President Nixon] emphasized that you have to face the fact that the whole problem is really the blacks. The key is to devise a system that recognizes this while not appearing to." –H.R. Haldeman, Nixon's Chief of Staff

Try as I might to stay away from the race issue, I'm finding it very hard to talk about the influence that the spirit of vengeance has on the American criminal justice system without recognizing that race plays a vital part as the target of the Social Control Agenda.

As we take a look back at the history of this country, we will see that people of color have been the target of this agenda which was driven by the white majority's resoluteness to target, to control, and to harass the minority! Through the laws that were enacted to impede progress and prevent advancement, the white majority sought to control those who they felt undeserving of being recognized as citizens, therefore keeping them ineligible to actively participate in the pursuit of the rights that are inherent to them as citizens of this country.

In the past these laws were enforced by the threat of and the administering of violence. But as time progressed they were enforced by more sophisticated means. These unjust laws empower the process of marginalization. They were set in place to identify, to relegate, and to confine to second class status, a part of society that the white majority and those who are in authority considered to be less important.

NATIVE AMERICANS

We can trace these unjust laws all the way back to the colonization of North America and the marginalization of the North American Indians. The taking of their land through force, coercion, and deceit was justified by laws that were derived from the belief in the theory of Manifest Destiny.

Unjust laws like the Indian Removal act of 1830 signed into law by then President Andrew Jackson, the Indian Appropriations Acts of 1851, 1871, 1885, and 1889. The Dawes Act of 1887 and the Burke act of 1906, along with the silly notion of "civilizing" the Indians by eliminating their culture through taking their children and teaching them white culture. They were also victims of slavery and the slave trade and ultimately were forced from their land and place on reservations. In 1838, 4000 Cherokee Indians died on the way to the reservation. That journey that they took was given the name the, "Trail of Tears.," They were the targets of the Social Control Agenda before social control became a catch phrase! They were the victims of unjust laws; created by those in authority pushing an unjust agenda.

ASIAN AMERICANS

In my research for the preparation of this book and during its writing, I was reminded of the extents that the white majority will go to maintain social control. With the precision of a microscope, they can and have magnified their intent on holding their target down by simply adjusting the focus of these unjust laws. Asian victimization is just one of the examples. The laws that were past lead to one of the most vengeful and embarrassing acts in the history of this nation!

We owe a great deal of appreciation to the Chinese laborers who contributed in what has been considered to be one of the greatest American technological feats of the nineteenth century. This accomplishment is the building of the Transcontinental Railroad. Instead, they became the victims of a vengeful society who saw them as undeserving of the rights that are inherent from being a human, and because of that they were deemed unworthy to be given the opportunity for citizenship in this country.

They gained favor for their work ethic, yet when the surface gold began to dry up at Sutter's Mill in Coloma, California during the gold rush they were blamed for it. That was the catalyst of the Chinese Exclusion Act signed into law on May 8, 1882, the Scott Act of 1888, and the Gary Act in 1892. However, the first unjust law with anti-Asian sentiment was the Page act of 1875. It included not only people from China but also Japan and people from all other Asian countries that wanted to come to the United States to work.

Right after the bombing of Pearl Harbor, Franklin D. Roosevelt the 32nd President of the United States signed executive order 9066 on February 19th, 1942. That order gave the U.S. military the authority to created "exclusion zones", and also declared all Japanese people excluded from those areas. From March 2nd, 1942 to May 3rd, 1942 a series of public proclamations were made and executive order 9095 was also signed by the President. Those actions would eventually culminate in the illegal detainment and forced relocation of approximately 120,000 Japanese Americans and Japanese nationals.

MEXICAN AMERICANS

The Mexican-American War was fought from 1846-1848, The Treaty of Guadalupe-Hidalgo expanded the United States control over a wide range of territory once belonging to Mexico. With the annexation of Texas in 1845, and the Gadsden Purchase in 1853, the treaty gave us what is now New Mexico, Colorado, Utah, Nevada, Arizona, and California.

Although the treaty promised that all Mexicans who owned land prior to the U.S. acquiring these territories would enjoy full protection as if they were American citizens, many of them lost their property in state and federal court because of unjust laws that were passed after that treaty. They were forced to leave and live under exclusionary standards similar to Jim Crow. From 1929 to 1939 the government of the United States sponsored the Mexican Repatriation movement. This was supposed to be voluntary, yet almost all of the 500,000 people that were deported were forced to leave and not given a choice. In 1954 the United States Immigration and Naturalization Service, (INS), launched Operation Wetback; a quasi-military operation to remove one million illegal immigrants for the southwestern United State. The problem with that was that the majority of the people that were forcefully removed were American citizens by birth.

The lynching of Mexican Americans and nationals is very hard to track for some reason, but are an egregious act stemming from the unjust laws of the Social Control Agenda. The actual amount of lynchings is unknown. It has been estimated that 597 Mexicans were lynch between the years of 1842-1928. Here again is another indictment on the vindictive nature of the white majority, and the unjust laws they conceived.

AFRICAN AMERICANS

Overall the largest target of the Social Control Agenda has been African Americans. Some of the unjust laws that were leveled at them may be the same as the ones leveled at other minority groups, however; the intensity, the fervor, the hatred and vindictiveness spent on them far exceeds the others! And sadly, the more things change, the more they stay the same!

From slavery and the slave trade that predates the Civil War, isolation through Jim Crow laws that lasted from 1800-1966 and the Black Codes that lasted from 1876-1965, to legalized voter disenfranchisement that was only over turned forty eight years ago, as-well-as the anti-miscegenation laws of 1863 that were put in place to ban interracial marriage and sexual relations between blacks and whites primarily however they also included a ban on interracial blending of any kind until 1967. Marginalized by the deceptive and oppressive policies of Segregation that allowed them to have their own neighborhoods, businesses, schools, services, and public accommodations that were inferior to what the white majority had. The "Lily White Movement" received its moniker in the late 19th century and remained relevant, (primarily in the south but had a large amount of influence nationwide) until the early 20th century; drove blacks from the Republican Party as well as political office by calling for and getting a ban against blacks from voting and holding political office based on the color of their skin!

From the lynching's and mob violence of the past, to the wrongful convictions, racial profiling and the disparity of today, the Social Control Agenda has left a lasting legacy of violence. Sadly with the unquenchable thirst for vengeance being the sole benefactor to the Social Control Agenda, the consequence has been that this selfish agenda has profited very little, if any profit has been gained at all!

Those who control the promulgation of the Social Control agenda have throughout the years tried to make sure that their way of life could not be threatened. The unjust laws they set in place served not only as measures of control, but as a foundation for them to build a false sense of security upon. Insecurity allows vengeance the opportunity to manifest itself. Fear and anxiety come from insecurity, which again is played on by those in authority. Who in turn create for the people a false sense of security by promising to keep their way of life safe with the enactment and enforcement of these unjust laws!

UNJUST THEN UNJUST NOW

That was then; this is now! The examples I have just described were laws enacted prior to the 1960's when Lady Justice stood up and rescinded most of them. In doing so, she became a victim of the Social Control Agenda herself through a military style coup that kid napped her and seated an imposter who gave vengeance a platform from which it was able to sabotage the criminal justice and created the unjust system that currently prevails.

Today these unjust laws are used in a more sophisticated way. They might appear to be less lethal now since they are not enforced through physical violence however; they are certainly more destructive then they were in the past. Why? Because this agenda utilizes a covert form of discrimination that has been the driving force behind the racial disparity that exists in the arrest, conviction, sentencing, and incarceration rates of the American criminal justice system. This proves the that in 1968 President Nixon and his administration found away to target "blacks" as he put it, as well as devise and conceal a plan to carry it out. That plan is called the Social Control Agenda.

Today the war on drugs has replaced the war on crime declared in the 1960's. Richard Nixon officially made that declaration in 1971. Later Ronald Reagan and his administration took the same approach in the 1980's that the Nixon administration did which was to target and control people of color and oppress them with a covert form of discrimination that was dubbed the "just say no" to drugs campaign, which was simply just another component of the Social Control Agenda. The huge disparity between the laws and sentencing for powder cocaine and crack or rock cocaine became the adjustments of magnification that were used to target and control people of color.

The laws that put small time pushers and users in prison as long as and sometimes longer then big time dealers opened up the flood gates of mass incarceration. Truth in sentencing, mandatory minimums sentencing, three strikes, and other policies continue to this day, (regardless of some reform), to rip and tear at the fabric of the African American community, as well as the Latino/Hispanic, the Asian, the American Indian, and the White communities in lesser degrees.

When it becomes more important to the majority to have their way of life preserved at any cost than to acknowledge that the minority are people and have rights too, then there you will find the vengeful Social Control Agenda alive and well. It is only when Lady Justice arrives on the scene to reform social control and she avails herself to all regardless of race, creed, color, and economic status; you will find true justice, and not just us!

The Social Control Agenda at its worst marginalizes the poor, the undereducated, the unemployed, and the addicted. Sadly, a high percentage of those I have just described are those Americans who are of African, Asian, Latino/Hispanic, and American Indian descent. However, I do need to convey to you that there is something encouraging about The Social Control Agenda.

Now I began this chapter by defining the concept of a law, as well as acknowledging the fact that without them there would certainly be anarchy. In other words our society would be in trouble if there were no laws to maintain control! Ah there it is! The encouraging thing about the Social Control Agenda is that it can maintain control and truly keep society safe, providing that the laws that are set in place include the concepts of fairness, impartiality, objectivity, and merit.

Protecting our society from those who are a threat will always be the right thing to do! However, when a people are targeted for the sole purpose of maintaining the upper hand, you can look as long as you want and try as hard as you like, but you will never find justice. What you will find though; shackled in the back seat of a police cruiser, indicted and convicted by a so called jury of their peers, and incarcerated in a jail or prison cell more often than those who have the advantage of the three C's: Color, Cash, and Credentials, is overwhelmingly, JUST US!

CHAPTER 11
JUSTICE WINS THE PEACE

Peace is not the absence of war; but the presence of justice.

Harrison Ford

What can we do as a nation to ensure that Justice can prevail? What do we do to reverse the unjust nature of the laws conceived to enforce the Social Control Agenda? For who has not been effected by our current criminal justice system? Incidentally; why should we seek to reform this broken system and why should we even care?

Who, what, where and why! These are the four questions we need to answer in order to fix this broken and archaic system and pull this nation back from the brink of destruction. Once we consider the amount of lives that have been wasted, at the very least, we have to recognize that there is an imbalance on the scales that symbolize justice in this nation. That being the case, we can say for certain that vengeance is now prevailing.

Having to acknowledge that fact will not make some of the law makers very happy!

Though some would agree with me and other advocates of change privately, the majority of them will openly be proud of the fact that they think they've done their job well! Nevertheless, these questions still remain and they need to be answered!

WINNING THE WAR BY WINNING THE PEACE

In the campaign prior to his 2nd term, and even more so during the last years of President George W. Bush's administration, there were serious questions and concerns as to how we could win the wars in Iraq and Afghanistan. From 1989 through the present, the United States Army War College sponsors a strategy conference which addresses the major security issues that are relevant to the United States, its allies, and the entire world. In 2004 the theme of this conference was; "*Winning the war by, Winning the peace": Strategy's for conflict and post-conflict in the 21st century.* Most of the focus was on these five major issues.

(1). How to fight an asymmetric war. (2). How to win the hearts and minds of the enemy populace. (3). How to terminate wars and develop exit strategies successfully. (4). How to counter weapons of mass destruction. (5). How to conduct urban combat successfully. Since those in power have declared war on crime and drugs, I would like to draw parallels between the military and law enforcement, take the focuses from the 2004 conference and apply them to one of the most violent internal conflicts in American history.

THE WHAT

The "what" that we can do to ensure that justice prevails is to realize that to win the war on crime and drugs we must do it by winning the peace! Armed with that revelation we can use it to effectively fight an asymmetric war!

Ecclesiastes 9:11 says in part that the *"race is not to the swift, nor the battle to the strong"*. In other words: When it pertains to war, just because you are bigger and better does not mean that you are going to win! For the definition of an asymmetric war is this: *"A conflict between two belligerents whose military power, strategy, and tactics differ significantly."* We learned this great lesson after Korea, Vietnam, and the first Gulf war when we went to battle with an overwhelming advantage, yet did not come home with an overwhelming victory!

Let's draw parallels between those wars and the war on crime and drugs. In the past because they had access to automatic weapons the Federal, State, and Local law enforcement officials felt that the criminal element had the advantage. That changed thanks to the Social Control Agenda. With the spirit of vengeance influencing its policies, the law makers took money that was budgeted for the social safety net and diverted it to the war on crime and drugs. They added more man power, more law enforcement agencies, and more sophisticated weaponry.

They enacted more stringent laws that would lead to more arrests, more convictions, and much longer sentences. Which then lead to the building of more prisons, and ultimately was the spark that ignited what is now become known as the mass incarceration movement.

Additionally, they advanced this agenda by launching a media campaign that gave them the ability to greatly influenced public opinion and to reshape the concept of Justice in this nation. If you put all that together, you would venture to say that they went to war having an overwhelming advantage! Yet it goes without saying that there is not a hint of victory in sight. Why is that?

Well; the first lesson that needs to be learned about how to fight an asymmetric war is that you should not underestimate the enemy or this fundamental miss match will infect you with what I call Goliath syndrome. In the story of David and Goliath you have a 9 and a half foot giant wearing over 400 lbs of armory and weaponry, talking a lot of trash! Opposing him was a skinny teenager wearing a Sheppard's tunic, carrying a Sheppard's staff, a slingshot, and a pouch full of rocks! It would seem that the overwhelming advantage would have gone to the Giant! However, before the battle even got started, the giant got knocked out with a rock and was decapitated with his own sword! What an unconventional way to die!

Goliath's problem was that he did not want to win the peace! He and the Philistines wanted to completely eradicate the Israelite's and would accept nothing less. On the other hand, David was not afraid of the Philistines or the giant, and utilized unconventional warfare to defeat his opponent and infused his people with the same courage he had to go out and fight, and then ultimately win the war!

TODAY'S GOLIATH

I believe the Federal, State and Local law enforcement agencies are the Goliath of today! The difference is that today's Goliath not only wants to win the war, it also wants to win the peace! While their determination to eradicate crime and drugs in this country is a lofty yet praise worthy goal, the hypocrisy that this giant walks in while trying to do so has given him a bad reputation!

Years of enacting unjust legislation that targeted and marginalized people of color has cost this giant much more time, money, and effort then he ever intended to spend on this war, and the only thing he's gotten in return is militancy, resentment, and mistrust! On the other hand, adversity has given today's David courage and helped him developed the strategy to unleashed a type of unconventional warfare that has made him victorious in many battles up to this point, and at the very least kept him in the fight.

TODAY'S DAVID

Today's David knows he is out manned, out gunned, and out financed yet he continues with overwhelming success to win this war with a series of head shots that has flattened every giant that the local, state and federal law makers have sent his way. Each and every time he decapitates one, another one takes its place. That leads to the question; "How is today's David winning this war?" The answers lies in what he is carrying in his pouch!

The rocks today's David carries as a part of his unconventional arsenal are equivalent to the "IED's" that the Army and Marines in Iraq and Afghanistan faced. These "IED's" are the secret deals he has made with people in high places! How do you think these drugs are getting into this country? And why do you think he has gotten away with what he's been doing for so long?

The facts that were proven and used as evidence by investigative reporter Gary Webb and chronicled in his book, *Dark Alliance: the*

CIA, the Contras, and the Crack Cocaine Explosion, made it very clear to all that the conspiracies were real and I believe still are in effect today. How can you fight a war on drugs when you are complicit in the importation, manufacturing, distribution, and the sale of the illegal drugs that you say are to blame for the exploding crime rate in this country? How can you win this war in the face of this kind of hypocrisy? You must do it by first winning the Peace!

THE WHERE

Where do we start to reverse the unjust nature of the laws that were conceived to enforce the Social Control Agenda? Where it all began! As a nation we must start with the narcissistic notion of Manifest Destiny, which is the belief that the United State was ordained by God to expand across the North American Continent. The problem with that was that racial superiority not Divine providence drove that notion. So the first thing we need to do is to reverse racial superiority by removing all racial designations! In so doing, there cannot be a majority, therefore no sense of superiority when we all are one. Are we not all American by birth or naturalization? However, the U.S. Government through the Census still bolsters the walls of division in this country by asking specifically for your race.

I understand why, but we as a nation must start here for the specific reason that I wrote about in the previous chapter. That reason is that race is the target of the Social Control Agenda. Consequently, racial injustice has created nationwide an enemy populace whose hearts and minds need to be won! How do you win the war in the streets of the cities where drugs and crime have taking the worst toll and caused the most damage? Where the devastating effects of marginalization are so demoralizing that the people living in those areas believe that they were sent there to die? You do that by first winning the Peace!

THE WHO

Who has not been affected by our current criminal justice system? At the end of 2007 the U.S. prison population: those in jail, in prison, on parole, or on probation totaled 7.3 million, or 1 in every 31 adults. This means that you are someone, or you know someone, or you know someone that knows someone, who is directly affected by our current criminal justice system. The United States of America has 5% of the world's population. How ironic is it that we as a nation houses 25% of the world's prisoners. POW's caught in a war where the casualty numbers far exceed the American service members who died in battle in Korea, Vietnam, and both Golf wars combined!

How can we put an end to this war? How can we develop a successful exit strategy that will reform the concept of the Social Control Agenda and still maintain social control? How can these reforms change the hearts and minds of an enemy populace that was created by their government through this unjust agenda? You must do it by first winning the peace!

THE WHY

Why should we seek to fix this broken system and why should we even care? The most important reason is to counter the effects of the WMD's that today's David and Goliath have launched in this nation. Tragically, the people that walk the streets of the cities where the weapons have caused the most devastation have been stripped of all hope because their opportunities for advancement have decreased, as their opportunities for retreat have increased exponentially.

Combine the effects that poverty, crime, illegal and prescription drugs have had in those areas, with the effects of all that the, "get tough on crime and drug," campaigns entail, along with the effects of a phenomenon called punitive justice, and what we have in this nation is a fallout larger than the ones felt after the Atomic bombs were dropped on Hiroshima and Nagasaki, Japan!

Wait a minute! I just heard someone ask, "Why should we even care?" I will excuse the selfish nature of that question and make my answer as selfless as possible. The reason why we should care is because it's the right thing to do! When you see your brother or sister down you are suppose to lend them a hand! Caring turns you into a listener and causes you to hear the pain of those in need. Then when we find out what they need the most, it will help us to conduct urban combat more effectively, and gain the initiative in the battle to win their hearts and minds! However, we can only get this done by first winning the peace!

WINNING THE PEACE

In a 1961 speech to the graduating class of the U.S. Naval Academy, President John F. Kennedy challenged the military leaders of the future by saying, *"You must know everything you can know about military power, and you must also understand the limits of military power. You must understand that few of the important problems of our time have, in the final analysis, been finally solved by military power alone."* In other words; you must know all the ins and outs of what you are called to do, but understand that your calling can't solve every problem by itself!

Knowing all the ins and outs of what you are called to do will make you less likely to abuse the amount of power that will be at your disposal. Having the understanding that what you are called to do cannot and will not solve every problem by itself keeps you humble and makes you receptive to the ideas, the guidance, the insight, and the cooperation of those who are called alongside you, as well as the variety of new technologies developed to expedite the solving of these problems.

I believe that knowledge is power! I also believe that understanding is authority: the proper administration of power. Knowledge and understanding are the essence of Justice, and when Justice is a part of the strategy for war; then you stand a better chance to end the conflict or at least develop a successful exit strategy. Because when Justice is the sole benefactor, the benefit will be peace!

Consequently, what we as a nation must finally understand is that our current strategy for the war on crime and drugs must change. We cannot continue to do the same things and expect to get different results! We must take a hard look at the evidence and realize that the only benefit that can be received from this strategy is the detriment from more conflict simply because vengeance was and still is the sole benefactor.

Punitive justice does not bring peace! It is an unbalanced and unjust attempt to end this asymmetric war by brute force. It is a weapon of attrition used in an unwinnable war and a failed alternative to acknowledging the wars futility, admitting defeat, and developing and implementing a successful exit strategy. The rightness of the punishment has been negated by its excessive nature and there is nothing to balance out the scales that symbolize justice because punishment is its only way to address the problem.

BALANCING THE SCALES

To balance out the scales that symbolize Justice, the concept of Justice in this nation must be redirected. If we are to win the peace we must understand the times that we live in, as well as acknowledge fact that conflict is a byproduct of human nature. The Bible calls this the end times and it is signified by internal and external struggle. Matt 24:6-7 says, *"And you shall hear of wars and rumors of wars. See that you are not troubled; for all these things must come to pass, but the end is not yet. For nation shall rise against nation, and kingdom against kingdom."*

I said all this to say that in the times we live in, understanding that true Justice brings peace in the midst of conflict is essential if we are to win this war or at the very least develop a successful exit strategy. In other words as it pertains to crime and drugs we must realize that because of the imperfect nature of man drugs and crime will always exist. That does not mean we should not pursue true justice!

We can win the peace even if we can't win the war if Justice prevails. For Justice to prevail, we must balance the scales of justice with absolute truth! The absolute truth sees no color and it only hears what is relevant to each case, so that when it pronounces judgment it will speak peace into the life of both the victim and the perpetrator. Punishment tempered in absolute truth will settle the conflict that vengeance creates and bring it to an end, or at least help to develop a successful exit strategy for the victim to move on and someday forgive and ultimately receive closure. Simultaneously it will allow the perpetrator to serve out his sentence without having to experience the mental torment that the spirit of vengeance unleashes because he will not have to live the rest of his life in state of disenfranchisement!

This is the kind of peace that we seek! For once we win that peace we will be able to look back and see that in the midst of conflict the system was changed. We will see that the system changed as we accumulated knowledge and gained understanding. We will see that justice gave us an authority that we could not abuse, for we tempered punishment in absolute truth. We will see that with absolute truth the rightness of punishment could not be negated, because it settled the conflict that vengeance created. We will look back and realize that because justice was the sole benefactor to this change, the benefit that we received from this change was peace!

CHAPTER 12
JUSTICE SUPREME

Having weighed all the evidence that has been laid out within the pages of this book, we can make the determination that vengeance is not Justice! However; Justice in its supremacy has the capacity for retribution. In fact it is the expectation of society that if a person resists the temptation of vigilantism, the legal system will take up their cause and prosecute the perpetrator not to the fullest extent of the law, but to the extent that the law requires. Then and only then can the punishment fit the crime and the victims see true Justice served.

We must understand that even in a day when the cry for vengeance is at an all time high that Justice alone reigns supreme! When the supremacy of Justice presides over a case there is no denying whose words have more power! For proper authority can't be usurped when it thrives in an atmosphere that was created by and established in absolute truth!

With that said; it is an absolute truth that the words of just legislation can supersede the angry diatribes of vengeance attempting to maintain the status quo. It is an absolute truth that the supremacy of Justice will exercise its authority over vengeance's attempt to provoke a verdict based on human emotions by using just words to masterfully create an atmosphere conducive for a conviction or exoneration to be adjudicated based on the merit of each case!

It is an absolute truth that a just sentence can endure language that seeks to exploit legal loop wholes on appeal because it was spoken with the voice of reason and articulated in a way that all who hear it understands that the sentence was established by a preponderance of the evidence. That by the way is what truly makes Justice supreme. So regardless of how loud the cry for vengeance gets, Justice's supremacy will always have the last word!

Here in lies the problem! If Justice always gets the last word, why then does vengeance seem to have more influence? It is because emotions drown out logic. The pain of being victimized exerts more influence on the legal system today because it focuses on the retributive part of Justice's supremacy. This does not in any way negate that supremacy; it only confirms society's misconception of what Justice truly is.

For over forty years justice served has been defined by the amount of punishment that we can administer, instead of meting out the appropriate sentence to match the criminal act. This is not true Justice because it neither has the authority to win the peace nor provides the opportunity to end the war and or develop a successful exit strategy. With the safety of our communities at issue, society would do better if we understood that Justice served means not only to lock them up, it also means that we should release them with the momentum to succeed!

In other words society's view of criminal justice has to include the reintegration of people who have spent time behind bars! Why is that you might ask! Because the supremacy of Justice has, (like the river that carved out the Grand Canyon,) cut through the bed rock of the unjust laws and exposed the depth of the hypocrisy, the width of the disparity, and the lengths that those who trust in the Social Control Agenda would go to control the people they felt they're better than!

JUSTICE ESTABLISHED

"We the people, in order form a more perfect union; establish justice" These are the first words in the Preamble of the American Constitution. In the heart beat of a people that desired to be free from the tyranny of a King and establish their own nation was an inherent understanding that to be a great nation Justice would have to be established.

They truly understood that without the establishment of Justice; there would not be a more perfect union, domestic tranquility would not be insured, the common defense would not be provided for, the general welfare would not be promoted and the blessings of liberty would not be secured!

They understood that "government of the people, by the people, and for the people," not the dictates of a monarch would build them a foundation that could stand the test of time and endure the attack from any enemy who would challenge their right to be called a nation!

They understood that fair and objective adjudication would give all of its citizens the freedom to engage in their inalienable rights without fear, because they understood that the supremacy of Justice would stand up to protect those rights. Ultimately; they understood that the cornerstone of this nation would always be the supremacy of Justice!

The establishment of Justice meant that its supremacy was intended to last forever. Solemnized by the signing of the Constitution the ten amendments called the Bill of Rights gave Justice that supremacy and from the time of its ratification until this nation ceases to exist, Justice would always oversee the affairs of this nation. Because at its core is the belief that all men were created as equals when it came to those inalienable rights.

However; as the years progressed the supremacy of Justice took a back seat to the provocation of human emotions. It is clear that a people who endured so much to gain their independence from a tyrant, became tyrants themselves. For the pages of the history book of this nation are covered with the fingerprint of the spirit of vengeance, and stained with the blood, sweat and tears of both its victim and its perpetrators. Why? Because like a ping pong player uses his paddle, vengeance uses human emotions as an instrument of retaliation.

REESTABLISHING JUSTICE

220 years after the ratification of the United States Constitution, whose purpose was to set limits on what the federal government could and could not do in regards to our personal liberties, there is a call throughout the land for the reestablishment of Justice. Many state and federal statues appear on the surface to be just however, they violate our personal liberties. The fear is that the broadening of the scope of these laws to gain the initiative in the war on drugs, crime, and now the war on terror, will cross the line and infringe on the rights of law abiding citizens.

In a nation built on the supremacy of Justice that is very important. However, just as important is the excessive amount of power that is being used on those who break the law. I repeat, "Don't do the crime if you can't do the time", but make the punishment fit the crime. Additionally, let that sentence bring closure to victim so that they can be healed as well as relief to the offender so that they can pursue a new life without having to face the obstacles that felony disenfranchisement laws and the collateral consequence sanctions create once they have been released.

The good thing is that Justice because of its supremacy has reestablished itself over and over again! It moves at the speed of change, and although changes is not always manifested immediately, once its fruit begins to bloom it serves in perpetuity. In other words, when something happens that causes a shift in the direction, momentum, or the dynamic of an institution, that shift will last forever.

That means that the Bill of Rights serves in perpetuity as the foundational change or the shift in the dynamic that united a people and helped inspired them to establish a new nation. Laws were enacted at all levels of government as this country grew however, not all of these laws were compliant with that foundational change. But because the Bill of Rights was established as Justice Supreme, regardless of the amount of time it takes, it eventually will bring into conformity every law that seeks to usurp that authority.

Today as a nation we are looking at how to reshape our concept of Justice. The truth of the matter is that this was inspired by the supremacy of Justice itself! When Lady Justice took back the seat at the bench of adjudication, she cut off the supply of vengeance and now our society is getting sober! Knowing that this nation could not survive any longer by self medication, Justice reestablished itself and injected its supremacy back into the blood stream of the criminal justice system to break our mental addiction. Breaking this country's mental addiction is the only place to start!

FREE YOU'RE MIND AND THE REST WILL FOLLOW

Although the need for vengeance will never die, its influence will diminish in the face of the supremacy of Justice. As that happens, the measure of safety in our country will grow because of three things. (1.) The reliance upon the supremacy of Justice to stand up and protect citizens as they engage in their inalienable rights. (2.) The knowledge that those who break the law cannot argue against the rightness of their punishment because of the supremacy of Justice. (3.) When those who have served their sentence are released back into society they will have received the proper instruction as well as obtained the knowledge that the obstacles they will face will be fewer and can be overcome thanks to and because of the supremacy of Justice.

It is easier to enjoy walking down the street when you don't have to worry about becoming a victim of a crime. It is easier to stay out of trouble when the stigma of being an ex-offender is lifted and you truly get a second chance at life! It is easier to forgive and forget, get healed and move on when the punishment fits the crime and you feel like justice has been served. It is easier for society to except the concept of the presumption of innocence when vengeance cannot use the media to promote its agenda because of the supremacy of Justice. This kind of freedom comes from the blanket of assurance that can only be provided by the supremacy of Justice. It is the peace that will free your mind, and when your mind is free, the rest of you will be free as well!

Free your mind from antiquated thinking that keeps you from accepting change and your hands will be free to take hold of the opportunities that change will bring. Free your mind from the fear that cripples your ability to move and your feet will be free take you to the places you've always wanted to go. Free your mind from doubt and negativism and your heart will be free to show you how to love again. "Free your mind and the rest will follow!"

"A mind is terrible thing to waste." That is the slogan from the ad campaign sponsored by the United Negro College Fund and the Ad Council in support of getting an education. Launched in 1972 it continues to be relevant 40 years later. For we need to be educated about the history of the Social Control Agenda so we do not make the same mistakes again.

Everyone who commits a crime is not a danger to society! As in each and every case there are both mitigating and aggravating circumstances that increase or decrease the severity of a criminal act and are indicators that help gauge the potential for the offender to change or to re-offend. No one should be punished for the rest of their life if it is not warranted! When we as a society get freed from that mindset, grace and forgiveness will definitely follow, and those offenders who have earned it will get the second chance that they deserve because of the supremacy of Justice. However; Justice can't be served when we've got vengeance on our mind!

CONCLUSION

I'd like to end this book the same way that I started it by quoting the second stanza of the theme song from the 1970's hit T.V. series Baretta, "Don't do the crime if you can't do the time!" Why? Because I'd like to send a clear message to and through everyone who reads this book that while I am an advocate for criminal justice reform; I am in no way soft on crime!

In fact, I believe in a form of criminal justice where the punishment that is meted out is one that is swift, remedial, and one that is commensurate to the type of crime that was committed! I believe in a form of criminal justice that does not incarcerate everyone that breaks the law but at the same time does not provide cable television for those that it does!

I believe in a form criminal justice in which a victim of a crime is avenged, but is never permitted to be the avenger! In other words; one in which a victims emotions have limited influence on the outcome of the trial and one that does not allow vengeance to use those emotions to shackle the perpetrator and keep them in bondage for the rest of their life!

I believe in a form of criminal justice in which the focus of the war on crime and drugs is not a people but a problem! Now some folks might say that people truly are the problem however; although I believe that there are evil people in this world and the ultimate reason for crime in this country is human weakness, punishment without provision has been proven to be a major contributor to recidivism and the escalating crime statistics!

I believe in a form of criminal justice that scoffs at the notion that anyone would have the unmitigated gall to stand in a court of law and expect a free pass simply because they have money, a lighter skin tone, or a position of power, or that a system would be designed to show bias towards those who are poor, have a darker skin tone, and are not as important!

I believe in a form of criminal justice that endorses the concept, enforces the precept, and embraces the philosophy of the equality of justice! One that believes that justice is truly for all! Because unfortunately "justice for all" as a policy has meant nothing more to the people in this nation than just being the closing phrase in the pledge of allegiance which is only recited by children every morning before the start of elementary school! It goes without saying that for the most part justice in America has only been for a privileged few!

JUSTICE FOR ALL

Justice for all means that no one gets away with breaking the law, that a crime must be adjudicated the same way across the board and that punitive efficacy is in place! Punitive efficacy is a method in which the punishment serves the dual purpose of protecting society and deterring would be criminals through the practice of egalitarian sentencing policies.

This would mean that the draconian laws on the books today do not have to be changed, they have to be thrown out and we as a nation have to enact new and just laws that are all inclusive! Because if "what is good for the goose, is good for the gander," then it would stand to reason that what justice is for one, should be and ultimately is justice for all!

With that being said; there is no need for another panel to be put together and waist time and money to tell us what's wrong with this system when we already know! What we need is the courage to stand up and confess our sins, admit to our prejudices, and take responsibility for our actions before the form of criminal justice that I believe in can become a reality and bring strength to a criminal justice system possessed by the spirit of vengeance!

In other words; reformation must come through reputation! Simply put this means that when we are able to step up to the plate of responsibility and show that our hearts and minds have change toward the way we deal with each other, then we will have a reason to believe that "justice for all" can in full demonstration be experienced in America!

The reputation of the American criminal justice system is one of target and control! It should be one of protection and deterrent! The methods that are used in this type of system awards us the distinction of being the most punitive country in the world. What's so ironic is that truthfully we are not as violent as it would seem. In fact violent crime and crime in general has been in decline in recent years, yet anywhere we go in the world our reputation precedes us!

The catalyst for changing our reputation is through internal diagnostics! For when you can look at yourself and admit your faults, your future will be bright and good success is eminent because change is on the horizon! On the other hand if you look at yourself and you deny that there are problems, refuse to accept change, and try to cover up your indiscretions like we have for so long, then what you will end up with is a system that is on the verge of blowing up in your face!

Fortunately it's not too late. After years of procrastination, policy makers are slowly moving towards reform, and are dismantling this punitive justice juggernaut to balance federal, state and local budgets. Why? Because the cost of mass incarceration has a serious chock- hold on our economy!

Advocates for and against social control rang in 2012 with the consensus that to reform criminal justice in the United States we need to cut cost through alternative sentencing policies for all non-violent offenses. Drug treatment, Electronic Surveillance, as-well-as a whole host of Community Control measures seems to be more cost effective than the warn out mass incarceration model. Unfortunately; this model is not intended to deal with our propensity for vengeance! It only allowed it to seek other avenues to gain more access in and more influence on our society! Guess what? It found one!

Recently there has also been a big push for prison privatization. The problem is that this for profit industry lobbies congress at both the state and federal levels for the enactment of more unjust laws and stricter policies that maintain the Social Control Agenda and keep people locked up longer so that they can reach their profit margins! Mass incarceration has been a multi-billion dollar industry where the spirit of vengeance reigns supreme! And as more and more states as well as the Federal Government move toward contracting with or outright selling prisons to private companies, I realize that what they are doing has nothing to do with bringing down the incarceration rate! The only thing they're doing is strengthening the spirit of vengeance's grip on this nation's criminal justice system in the name of fiscal responsibility!

Vengeance desires to become the CFO of this criminal justice juggernaut! Now if we allow it to; it will combine the propensity for retribution by the victim and society with the propensity for greed in corporate America and that will drive us over the brink of destruction! Look out people! You've been warned! Justice can't be served we've got vengeance and they've got greed on their mind!

www.ingramcontent.com/pod-product-compliance
Lightning Source LLC
Chambersburg PA
CBHW051714170526
45167CB00002B/655